Functional Programming in JavaScript:

Building Reliable, Reusable, and Scalable Applications with
Functional Paradigms

Matthew D.Passmore

TABLE OF CONTENTS

PART I: INTRODUCTION TO FUNCTIONAL PROGRAMMING IN JAVASCRIPT

Chapter 1
Understanding Functional Programming

What Is Functional Programming?
Benefits of Functional Programming
Functional Programming vs. Object-Oriented Programming
Key Concepts in Functional Programming

Chapter 2
JavaScript Fundamentals for Functional Programming

JavaScript as a Multi-paradigm Language
Understanding JavaScript Functions
Immutability in JavaScript

First-class and Higher-order Functions

Chapter 3
Functional Principles and Best Practices

Avoiding Side Effects
Writing Pure Functions
Embracing Immutability
Using Composition over Inheritance

PART II: CORE FUNCTIONAL CONCEPTS IN JAVASCRIPT

Chapter 4
Higher-order Functions

What Are Higher-order Functions?
Common Higher-order Functions (map, filter, reduce)
Using Higher-order Functions in JavaScript

Chapter 5: Closures and Lexical Scoping

Understanding Closures in JavaScript

Practical Applications of Closures

Scope and Lexical Binding

Chapter 6

Recursion in Functional Programming

Basics of Recursion

Implementing Recursive Functions in JavaScript

Tail Call Optimization

Avoiding Common Pitfalls in Recursion

PART III: ADVANCED FUNCTIONAL TECHNIQUES

Chapter 7

Function Composition

What Is Function Composition?

Composing Functions in JavaScript

Using compose and pipe Functions

Chapter 8
Currying and Partial Application

Introduction to Currying
Implementing Currying in JavaScript
Benefits of Currying and Partial Application

Chapter 9
Functors and Monads

Understanding Functors in JavaScript
The Concept of Monads
Practical Use Cases for Functors and Monads

PART IV: FUNCTIONAL PATTERNS AND
APPLICATIONS

Chapter 10
Error Handling in Functional Programming

Error Handling Strategies

Using Either, Maybe, and Option Types

Handling Errors Functionally in JavaScript

Chapter 11

Functional Design Patterns

Strategy Pattern

Command Pattern

Using Functional Patterns in JavaScript Applications

Chapter 12

Asynchronous Functional Programming

Promises and Functional Programming

Async/Await in Functional Code

Using Functional Patterns for Asynchronous Workflows

PART V: BUILDING APPLICATIONS WITH FUNCTIONAL PARADIGM

Chapter 13
 Building Reusable Components

Structuring Code for Reusability
Composing Components Functionally
Testing and Debugging Functional Code

Chapter 14
 State Management in Functional Applications

Functional Approaches to State
Managing State in Complex Applications
Using Libraries like Redux with Functional Patterns

Chapter 15
Functional Programming in Real-world JavaScript

Real-world Use Cases
Performance Considerations

Best Practices for Large-scale Functional JavaScript

PART I: INTRODUCTION TO FUNCTIONAL PROGRAMMING IN JAVASCRIPT

Chapter 1
Understanding Functional Programming

Functional programming is a programming paradigm that treats computation as the evaluation of mathematical functions, emphasizing the use of pure functions and immutability. Unlike imperative programming, which relies on changing state and explicit commands, functional programming aims to minimize side effects, making code more predictable, reusable, and easier to test.

In functional programming, functions are first-class citizens, meaning they can be passed as arguments, returned from other functions, and assigned to variables. This allows for techniques like higher-order functions, which take other functions as inputs or output new functions, promoting modular, reusable code. Functional programming also encourages the use of immutable data, which prevents variables from being altered after they're created, reducing unexpected changes in state and enhancing code stability.

By adopting functional programming in JavaScript, developers can build more reliable, scalable, and maintainable applications, especially as complexity grows.

What Is Functional Programming?

Functional programming (FP) is a paradigm in software development that centers around using functions to build programs. In FP, functions are treated as first-class entities, meaning they can be stored in variables, passed as arguments, or returned from other functions. This approach promotes writing code with "pure functions," which always produce the same output given the same input and do not cause side effects (changes in state outside the function).

Key principles of functional programming include immutability, where data is not changed after it's created, and declarative coding, which emphasizes describing what should be done rather than how to do it. By minimizing changes in state and avoiding side effects, FP makes code more predictable, easier to debug, and often simpler to test. Functional programming is especially useful for tasks requiring high reliability and modularity, making it popular for developing scalable and maintainable applications in JavaScript and beyond.

Benefits of Functional Programming

Functional programming (FP) offers several advantages that make it a valuable approach, especially for building reliable, scalable, and maintainable applications.

Improved Readability and Maintainability: FP encourages a declarative coding style, where code describes what is being done rather than how. This makes the code easier to read and understand, as functions tend to be small, focused, and descriptive, enhancing maintainability.

Enhanced Predictability with Pure Functions: Pure functions, a core concept in FP, always return the same output for the same input and don't modify any external state. This predictability makes functions easier to reason about, as they act independently, reducing potential bugs and unexpected behavior.

Easier Debugging and Testing: With minimal side effects and immutability, FP reduces complex interactions between components, making it easier to isolate and test functions individually. Testing becomes straightforward since each function's behavior depends solely on its inputs.

Better Modularity and Reusability: FP emphasizes composing smaller functions to perform complex tasks. This modular design means that functions can be reused across various parts of an application, reducing redundancy and increasing flexibility.

Simplified Concurrency: Since FP promotes immutability and avoids shared state, it's naturally suited to handle concurrent processing. By minimizing state changes, FP makes it easier to work with parallel or asynchronous processes, which can enhance application performance and scalability.

Reduced Error-Prone Code: Functional code that avoids mutable states and side effects is less likely to introduce hard-to-detect errors, making applications more stable and robust.

In JavaScript, adopting FP principles can lead to cleaner, more efficient code that scales effectively, making it a valuable approach for building complex, modern web applications.

Functional Programming vs. Object-Oriented Programming

Functional Programming (FP) and Object-Oriented Programming (OOP) are two popular programming paradigms with distinct approaches to building applications.

1. Core Philosophy

Functional Programming: FP treats computation as the evaluation of mathematical functions and emphasizes what is being computed. It focuses on immutability and pure functions, aiming to minimize side effects and changes in state.

Object-Oriented Programming: OOP is centered around objects, which combine data and methods into encapsulated units. It emphasizes how objects interact with each other, using inheritance, encapsulation, and polymorphism to organize and manage code.

2. Data and State Management

FP: Functional programming favors immutability, meaning data is not altered after it's created. Instead, new data structures are returned when changes are needed, enhancing predictability and reducing unintended side effects.

OOP: OOP typically relies on mutable state, where objects can change their properties over time. This mutable state can make it more challenging to track how data changes, especially in larger applications with numerous interdependencies.

3. Functions and Methods

FP: In FP, functions are first-class citizens. They can be assigned to variables, passed as arguments, and returned from other functions, allowing for flexible and modular code through techniques like higher-order functions and composition.

OOP: In OOP, methods (functions attached to objects) operate on the data contained within the objects. Behavior is usually associated with specific classes or instances, promoting an "action on object" approach rather than abstract function-based logic.

4. Modularity and Code Reusability

FP: FP promotes code reusability by composing small, pure functions that perform specific tasks. Since functions are isolated and don't rely on external state, they are easily reused across different contexts.

OOP: OOP achieves reusability through inheritance and polymorphism. Code can be extended by creating subclasses that inherit behavior, though this can lead to complexity as hierarchies grow and can sometimes make code harder to modify.

5. Concurrency and Parallelism

FP: FP's immutability and pure functions make it well-suited for concurrent or parallel processing since there is no need to worry about shared mutable state or race conditions. This makes FP ideal for applications that require high performance with concurrent tasks.

OOP: OOP can handle concurrency, but managing shared mutable state across objects can lead to complex issues, like deadlocks and race conditions, requiring careful use of synchronization.

6. Error Handling and Debugging

FP: With fewer side effects and immutable data, FP reduces unexpected behaviors, making code easier to test and debug. Since functions are pure and independent, their outputs are predictable, which simplifies identifying the source of errors.

OOP: OOP code can be harder to debug due to mutable states and interdependencies among objects. Errors in one part of the object hierarchy can propagate, making it challenging to isolate the cause without affecting other components.

Summary

FP is best suited for tasks requiring simplicity, predictability, and concurrent processing, making it popular for data transformations, functional UIs, and applications where immutability is advantageous.
OOP excels in applications where modeling real-world entities and their interactions is key, such as GUI applications and complex systems with numerous interrelated components.

Both paradigms have strengths and are often complementary. Many modern JavaScript applications adopt a hybrid approach, leveraging functional programming principles within object-oriented structures to maximize code readability, modularity, and performance.

Key Concepts in Functional Programming

Functional programming (FP) relies on a few foundational concepts that distinguish it from other paradigms. These principles promote writing clean, predictable, and modular code. Here are some of the key concepts:

1. Pure Functions

A pure function is a function that, given the same input, will always return the same output and does not produce side effects (i.e., it does not alter external state). This predictability makes pure functions easier to understand, test, and debug.
Example: A function that multiplies a number by two without modifying any external variables is a pure function.

2. Immutability

In FP, data is immutable, meaning it cannot be modified once created. Instead of changing data, new data structures are created with the desired changes, preserving the original data.
Immutability reduces bugs associated with state changes and makes applications more predictable, especially in concurrent programming.

3. First-Class and Higher-Order Functions

First-Class Functions: Functions are treated as "first-class citizens," meaning they can be assigned to variables, passed as arguments, and returned from other functions. This allows for more flexible and modular code.

Higher-Order Functions: A higher-order function is a function that takes other functions as arguments or returns a function as its result. Common examples include JavaScript's map, filter, and reduce functions, which allow operations on collections in a declarative way.

4. Function Composition

Function composition is the process of combining two or more functions to produce a new function. Instead of chaining operations or using complex loops, functions can be composed to build complex behavior from simpler ones, making code more readable and modular.

For instance, combining two functions, double (to multiply a number by 2) and square (to square a number), results in a new function that doubles and then squares its input.

5. Recursion

Recursion is a technique in which a function calls itself to solve a problem. In FP, recursion often replaces traditional looping constructs, as it aligns with the immutability principle by avoiding mutable loop counters.

Recursive functions can simplify code by breaking down problems into smaller instances of themselves, though careful handling is required to avoid excessive memory use in deeply recursive cases.

6. Closures

A closure is a function that "remembers" its lexical scope, even when the function is executed outside that scope. Closures enable functions to maintain references to the variables in their scope, providing a way to create private data or preserve state between function calls.

Closures are particularly useful in FP for creating functions with "remembered" configurations or parameters, allowing for flexible and reusable code.

7. Currying and Partial Application

Currying: Currying transforms a function with multiple arguments into a series of nested functions, each taking a single argument. For example, a function add(x, y) could be curried to add(x)(y).

Partial Application: Partial application is the process of fixing a few arguments of a function and returning a new function that takes the remaining arguments. This can simplify complex functions by breaking them down into simpler ones.

8. Lazy Evaluation

Lazy evaluation means delaying the computation of expressions until their values are needed. This can improve performance by avoiding unnecessary calculations, especially in large data processing.

JavaScript does not natively support lazy evaluation, but it can be simulated using techniques such as generators and promises.

9. Functor and Monad

Functor: A functor is a data structure (like an array) that can be mapped over, applying a function to each value inside without changing the structure. This helps keep code functional, preserving the context of data.

Monad: A monad is a more advanced concept used for handling side effects (e.g., handling asynchronous operations, errors) in FP. Monads provide a way to "wrap" values and define specific behaviors for working with them in a predictable way.

Summary

These core concepts of functional programming provide tools for creating modular, predictable, and reusable code. By understanding and applying these principles, developers can improve the reliability, readability, and scalability of their applications, especially in environments like JavaScript where functional paradigms are widely adopted.

Chapter 2

JavaScript Fundamentals for Functional Programming

JavaScript, while not a purely functional language, provides several features that make it suitable for functional programming (FP). Here are some foundational concepts in JavaScript that support FP:

1. First-Class Functions

In JavaScript, functions are first-class citizens, meaning they can be assigned to variables, passed as arguments, and returned from other functions. This flexibility enables the use of higher-order functions, a key feature in FP.

2. Higher-Order Functions

JavaScript allows functions to accept other functions as arguments or return them as values. Built-in functions like map, filter, and reduce are common higher-order functions used to process arrays in a functional way, promoting declarative, concise code.

3. Closures

Closures in JavaScript allow functions to access variables from their outer scope even after that scope has exited. Closures support encapsulation and data privacy, making them useful for creating flexible, reusable functions with internal state.

4. Immutability

Although JavaScript does not enforce immutability, developers can use techniques such as const declarations, Object.freeze(), and libraries like Immutable.js to maintain unchangeable data. This aligns with FP principles, reducing unintended side effects.

5. Pure Functions

JavaScript functions can be written as pure functions by ensuring they always produce the same output for the same input and avoid side effects. This makes the functions predictable and easier to test and debug.

6. Array Methods for Functional Operations

JavaScript's array methods (map, filter, reduce, every, some, etc.) allow developers to perform operations without mutating the original array, following the FP approach of data immutability.

7. Arrow Functions

Arrow functions provide a concise syntax for writing functions and support lexical this binding, which can simplify code and improve readability, especially in functional programming contexts.

8. Currying and Partial Application

JavaScript supports currying and partial application, techniques that allow functions to be broken down into smaller, reusable units. This is often achieved using libraries or custom helper functions.

By leveraging these JavaScript fundamentals, developers can apply functional programming principles to write cleaner, more modular, and maintainable code, making JavaScript a powerful language for both functional and hybrid programming styles.

JavaScript as a Multi-paradigm Language

JavaScript is a versatile, multi-paradigm programming language, meaning it supports multiple approaches to programming, including functional, object-oriented, and procedural paradigms. This flexibility makes JavaScript adaptable to a wide range of applications, from simple scripts to complex, scalable web applications.

1. Procedural Programming

Procedural programming in JavaScript involves writing sequences of instructions (procedures) that execute in order. This paradigm is useful for simple, linear tasks and emphasizes using functions to break down complex processes into manageable steps.

2. Object-Oriented Programming (OOP)

JavaScript provides robust support for OOP, allowing developers to create and manipulate objects with properties and methods. Using classes (introduced in ES6) or prototypes, developers can model real-world entities, encapsulate data, and establish relationships between objects. Concepts like inheritance, polymorphism, and encapsulation allow for building complex applications with reusable and modular code.

3. Functional Programming (FP)

JavaScript also supports functional programming, a paradigm that emphasizes pure functions, immutability, and higher-order functions. With functions as first-class citizens, JavaScript enables a functional approach through methods like map, filter, and reduce, as well as features like closures, arrow functions, and immutable data structures. FP is ideal for building predictable, modular, and testable code.

4. Event-Driven Programming

JavaScript is also highly suited for event-driven programming, especially in web development. The language's asynchronous nature allows it to handle events (like user clicks, form submissions, or data updates) without blocking the main execution flow. This makes JavaScript an effective choice for building responsive applications.

Benefits of a Multi-Paradigm Approach

By supporting multiple paradigms, JavaScript allows developers to choose the best approach for each task or combine approaches in a single application. This flexibility promotes creativity and adaptability, making it easier to tackle different types of problems.
For instance, a developer might use OOP to model the structure of a web application, FP for data transformations and side-effect-free functions, and event-driven programming for user interactions.

Conclusion

JavaScript's multi-paradigm nature is one of its greatest strengths, allowing it to meet the needs of various programming styles and application requirements. Developers can leverage this adaptability to create efficient, modular, and scalable code, enabling JavaScript's widespread use in modern web and mobile development.

Understanding JavaScript Functions

In JavaScript, functions are one of the core building blocks, serving as reusable chunks of code that can be invoked as needed. Functions allow developers to encapsulate logic, making code more modular, readable, and maintainable. JavaScript treats functions as first-class citizens, meaning they can be assigned to variables, passed as arguments, and returned from other functions. Here's an overview of JavaScript functions and their various types and features:

1. Function Declarations

A function declaration defines a named function and can be called before it's defined due to hoisting.

Example:
javascript
Copy code
function greet(name) {
**   return `Hello, ${name}!`;**
}

Function declarations are ideal when you want to define reusable code blocks in a clear and structured way.

2. Function Expressions

A function expression creates a function within an expression and assigns it to a variable. Unlike declarations, function expressions are not hoisted, so they must be defined before they are called.

Example:
javascript
Copy code
const greet = function(name) {

```javascript
    return `Hello, ${name}!`;
};
```

3. Arrow Functions

Introduced in ES6, arrow functions provide a shorter syntax for writing functions and use lexical this binding. They're commonly used for concise, inline functions but cannot be used as constructors.
Example:
javascript
Copy code
```javascript
const greet = (name) => `Hello, ${name}!`;
```
Arrow functions are ideal for functional programming and when using callbacks, as they allow for simpler code and maintain this context.

4. Higher-Order Functions

Higher-order functions are functions that accept other functions as arguments or return functions as results. They're essential in functional programming and commonly used with methods like map, filter, and reduce.

Example:

javascript
Copy code

```javascript
const numbers = [1, 2, 3];
const doubled = numbers.map(num => num * 2); // Output: [2, 4, 6]
```

5. Anonymous Functions

Anonymous functions are functions without a name, typically used as arguments for other functions. They're commonly used in callbacks and event handling.
Example:

javascript
Copy code

```javascript
setTimeout(function() {
    console.log("This is an anonymous function!");
}, 1000);
```

6. Immediately Invoked Function Expressions (IIFE)

An IIFE is a function that runs immediately after it's defined, often used to create a local scope and avoid polluting the global scope.

Example:
javascript
Copy code

```javascript
(function() {
    console.log("This function runs immediately!");
})();
```

7. Closures

A closure is a function that remembers its outer scope even when executed outside that scope. Closures allow data encapsulation and are helpful for creating private variables.
Example:

javascript
Copy code

```javascript
function createCounter() {
    let count = 0;
    return function() {
        count += 1;
```

```javascript
    return count;
  };
}
const counter = createCounter();
console.log(counter()); // Output: 1
```

8. Rest Parameters and Default Parameters

Rest Parameters: Allow functions to accept an indefinite number of arguments, stored in an array.

Default Parameters: Allow default values for parameters when arguments aren't provided.

Example:

javascript

Copy code

```javascript
function sum(...numbers) {
    return numbers.reduce((total, num) => total + num, 0);
}
function greet(name = "Guest") {
    return `Hello, ${name}!`;
}
```

9. Function Scope and this Binding

Functions in JavaScript have their own scope. The this keyword within a function refers to the function's execution context. In regular functions, this can vary based on how a function is called, but arrow functions have lexical this binding, capturing the this value from their surrounding scope.

Conclusion

JavaScript functions are versatile and essential for creating reusable, modular code. Understanding the different types and behaviors of functions, as well as concepts like closures and higher-order functions, enables developers to write cleaner, more efficient code. Functions not only allow encapsulation and reusability but also make JavaScript a powerful language for both procedural and functional programming.

Immutability in JavaScript

Immutability is a key concept in functional programming, and it refers to the idea that once a value is created, it cannot be changed. Instead of modifying the original value, new values are created with the desired changes. This principle encourages writing predictable and bug-free code by avoiding side effects and unintended mutations of data. While JavaScript does not enforce immutability by default, developers can use certain techniques and practices to adopt immutability in their code.

1. Why Immutability Matters

Predictability: When data is immutable, its value does not change throughout the program. This makes the program more predictable, as functions or operations that depend on immutable data will always produce the same result for the same inputs.

Debugging and Testing: Immutability reduces the complexity of debugging since the state of the data remains consistent. It's easier to track the flow of data and detect where things might go wrong.

Concurrency and Parallelism: Immutability is particularly useful in concurrent programming, where multiple processes may need to access and modify data simultaneously. Since immutable data cannot be changed, there is no risk of race conditions or data corruption.

Side Effect-Free Functions: Functional programming relies heavily on pure functions, which are functions that do not alter external state. By using immutable data, functions can operate without side effects, making the codebase cleaner and more reliable.

2. Immutability in JavaScript

While JavaScript's primitive types (such as strings, numbers, and booleans) are inherently immutable, objects and arrays are mutable by default. To implement immutability in JavaScript, developers need to follow certain strategies.

a. Using const for Variables

Declaring variables with const ensures that the reference to an object or array cannot be changed, although the content of the object/array can still be mutated. This does not fully enforce immutability but ensures that the reference to the variable cannot be reassigned.
Example:

javascript
Copy code

```javascript
const obj = { name: "Alice" };
obj = {}; // Error: Assignment to constant variable.
```

b. Using Object.freeze()

Object.freeze() is a method in JavaScript that makes an object immutable by preventing new properties from being added, existing properties from being removed, or properties from being modified. However, Object.freeze() only applies to the top level of the object. Nested objects are still mutable unless explicitly frozen.
Example:

```javascript
Copy code
const person = { name: "Alice", age: 25 };
Object.freeze(person);
person.age = 26; // This will fail silently or throw an error in strict mode
```

c. Spread Syntax (...) and Object/Array Destructuring

The spread syntax (...) allows developers to create a new object or array that is a shallow copy of an existing one. This is useful for making changes to an object or array without mutating the original.

Example (Arrays):

```javascript
Copy code
const arr = [1, 2, 3];
const newArr = [...arr, 4]; // arr remains unchanged
```

Example (Objects):

```javascript
Copy code
const person = { name: "Alice", age: 25 };
const newPerson = { ...person, age: 26 }; // person remains unchanged
```

d. Object.assign()

Object.assign() is used to create shallow copies of objects. It copies the values of all enumerable properties from one or more source objects to a target object. It doesn't affect the original object, ensuring that no mutation occurs.

Example:

javascript

Copy code
```
const person = { name: "Alice", age: 25 };
const updatedPerson = Object.assign({}, person, { age:
26 });
```

e. Immutable Data Structures (Libraries)

JavaScript does not provide built-in deep immutability, but libraries like Immutable.js and Mori offer persistent data structures (e.g., lists, maps) that ensure immutability at all levels. These libraries provide efficient ways to work with immutable collections.

Example using Immutable.js:

javascript
Copy code
```
const { Map } = require('immutable');
const person = Map({ name: 'Alice', age: 25 });
const updatedPerson = person.set('age', 26); //
Returns a new Map, leaving the original intact
```

3. Challenges of Immutability in JavaScript

Performance Considerations: Although immutability offers several benefits, it can sometimes lead to performance overhead when large data structures need to be copied. This can be mitigated with efficient libraries and techniques like persistent data structures.

Deep Immutability: While methods like Object.freeze() provide shallow immutability, deeply nested objects require additional handling to prevent accidental mutation. Libraries like Immutable.js solve this problem by providing deep immutability out of the box.

4. Best Practices for Immutability

Use const to prevent reassignment of references to objects or arrays.

Use the spread syntax (...) or Object.assign() to create copies of objects or arrays when making modifications.

Leverage libraries like Immutable.js for more advanced immutable data structures.

Always think in terms of creating new data rather than mutating the existing data, which aligns with the principles of functional programming.

Conclusion

Immutability is a powerful concept that promotes clean, maintainable, and predictable code. While JavaScript does not enforce immutability by default, developers can adopt techniques such as Object.freeze(), spread syntax, and libraries like Immutable.js to implement immutability. By adopting immutable practices, developers can avoid common pitfalls associated with mutable state, leading to more reliable and bug-free applications.

First-class and Higher-order Functions

JavaScript is a versatile, multi-paradigm language that supports functional programming. A key aspect of functional programming in JavaScript is the concept of first-class and higher-order functions. These features enable powerful techniques like callbacks, closures, and function composition, which are foundational to writing clean, reusable, and efficient code.

1. First-class Functions

A first-class function is a function that can be treated like any other variable. This means that functions in JavaScript can:

Be assigned to variables.
Be passed as arguments to other functions.
Be returned from other functions.
Be stored in data structures such as arrays or objects.
JavaScript treats functions as first-class citizens, allowing for a high degree of flexibility and enabling functional programming practices. Here's a brief breakdown of these capabilities:

a. Functions as Variables
Functions can be assigned to variables just like any other value (such as a string, number, or object).

Example:
javascript
Copy code
```
const greet = function(name) {
    return `Hello, ${name}!`;
};
console.log(greet("Alice")); // Output: Hello, Alice!
```

b. Passing Functions as Arguments

Functions can be passed as arguments to other functions, allowing for more dynamic and flexible behavior.

Example:
javascript
Copy code
```
function sayHello(name) {
    return `Hello, ${name}!`;
}

function greetPerson(greetingFunction, name) {
    console.log(greetingFunction(name));
}

greetPerson(sayHello, "Bob"); // Output: Hello, Bob!
```

c. Returning Functions from Other Functions

Functions can return other functions, creating closures and allowing for currying and function composition.

Example:

javascript

Copy code

```javascript
function multiplyBy(factor) {
  return function(number) {
    return number * factor;
  };
}

const double = multiplyBy(2);
console.log(double(5)); // Output: 10
```

d. Storing Functions in Data Structures

Functions can be stored in arrays, objects, or other data structures and accessed dynamically.

Example:

javascript

Copy code

```javascript
const operations = [
  (x, y) => x + y,  // addition
  (x, y) => x - y,  // subtraction
  (x, y) => x * y   // multiplication
```

```
];
```

```
console.log(operations[0](5,    3));   //   Output:   8
(addition)
console.log(operations[1](5,    3));   //   Output:   2
(subtraction)
```

2. Higher-order Functions

A higher-order function is a function that either:

Takes one or more functions as arguments, or
Returns a function as its result.
Higher-order functions are central to functional programming as they allow functions to be used in more flexible and abstract ways. Here are some common scenarios where higher-order functions are useful:

a. Functions that Accept Other Functions as Arguments

Higher-order functions can accept other functions as parameters, allowing for dynamic behavior and abstraction.

Example (with map):

javascript

Copy code

```
const numbers = [1, 2, 3];
const squared = numbers.map(function(num) {
    return num * num;
});
console.log(squared); // Output: [1, 4, 9]
```

Example (with custom higher-order function):

javascript

Copy code

```
function applyOperation(arr, operation) {
    return arr.map(operation);
}

const numbers = [1, 2, 3];
const result = applyOperation(numbers, function(num) {
    return num * num;
});
console.log(result); // Output: [1, 4, 9]
```

b. Functions that Return Other Functions

Higher-order functions can also return functions, enabling advanced techniques such as currying, function composition, and closures.

Example (function composition):
javascript
Copy code

```javascript
function compose(f, g) {
    return function(x) {
        return f(g(x)); // Returns the result of f(g(x))
    };
}

const add2 = (x) => x + 2;
const multiplyBy3 = (x) => x * 3;

const addThenMultiply = compose(multiplyBy3, add2);
console.log(addThenMultiply(5)); // Output: 21 ((5 + 2) * 3)
```

c. Common Higher-order Functions in JavaScript

JavaScript's array methods are examples of higher-order functions, such as map, filter, reduce, and forEach. These methods accept functions as arguments to perform operations on arrays.

map(): Creates a new array by applying a function to each element of the original array.

javascript
Copy code

```javascript
const numbers = [1, 2, 3];
const doubled = numbers.map((num) => num * 2);
console.log(doubled); // Output: [2, 4, 6]
```

filter(): Creates a new array with elements that pass a test defined by a function.

javascript
Copy code

```javascript
const numbers = [1, 2, 3, 4, 5];
const evenNumbers = numbers.filter((num) => num % 2 === 0);
console.log(evenNumbers); // Output: [2, 4]
```

reduce(): Applies a function to accumulate values in an array to a single result.

javascript
Copy code
const numbers = [1, 2, 3, 4];
const sum = numbers.reduce((acc, num) => acc + num, 0);
console.log(sum); // Output: 10

forEach(): Iterates over each element in an array and performs an operation (side effect).

javascript
Copy code
const numbers = [1, 2, 3];
numbers.forEach((num) => console.log(num * 2)); // Output: 2, 4, 6

3. Benefits of First-class and Higher-order Functions

Flexibility: First-class and higher-order functions enable dynamic and flexible code, where behavior can be passed, returned, and modified easily.

Code Reusability: Functions can be reused in different contexts by passing them as arguments or returning them as results.

Abstraction: Higher-order functions allow for the abstraction of common patterns, like transformations or aggregations, making code more concise and easier to maintain.

Functional Programming: These features enable key functional programming concepts such as currying, function composition, and declarative programming, helping developers write cleaner, more efficient, and less error-prone code.

Conclusion

First-class and higher-order functions are foundational concepts in JavaScript that unlock the full potential of functional programming. They allow for flexible, reusable, and highly abstracted code, leading to cleaner, more maintainable applications. By understanding and utilizing these concepts, JavaScript developers can write code that is both powerful and elegant.

Chapter 3

Functional Principles and Best Practices

Functional programming (FP) is a programming paradigm that treats computation as the evaluation of mathematical functions and avoids changing state or mutable data. Adopting functional principles and best practices can lead to cleaner, more maintainable, and predictable code. Here are the core principles and best practices for writing functional code in JavaScript:

1. Immutability

Immutability is the principle that once data is created, it cannot be modified. Instead of changing the data, you create new copies with the updated values. This approach prevents unintended side effects and helps make the code more predictable and easier to debug.

Best Practice: Use const to define variables and avoid mutating objects or arrays. Use techniques like the spread operator (...) or Object.assign() to create copies of data structures instead of altering them directly.

Example:

javascript
Copy code
```javascript
const user = { name: "Alice", age: 30 };
const updatedUser = { ...user, age: 31 }; // Creating a new object instead of modifying the original
```

2. Pure Functions

A pure function is one that always produces the same output for the same input and has no side effects. This means that pure functions do not modify any external state or variables.

Best Practice: Keep functions pure by avoiding reliance on global variables or modifying external state. Focus on returning results based solely on input arguments.

Example:
javascript

Copy code
```
const add = (a, b) => a + b; // Pure function, no side effects
```

3. First-Class Functions

In functional programming, functions are first-class citizens, meaning they can be passed as arguments, returned from other functions, and assigned to variables.

Best Practice: Use functions as arguments (callbacks) or return functions from other functions to enable greater flexibility and code reusability.

Example:
javascript
Copy code
```
const greet = (name) => `Hello, ${name}!`;
const sayHello = (greetingFunction, name) => console.log(greetingFunction(name));
sayHello(greet, "Alice");
```

4. Higher-Order Functions

Higher-order functions are functions that either take other functions as arguments or return functions. These enable abstraction and reduce code duplication.

Best Practice: Use higher-order functions like map, filter, reduce, and forEach to operate on collections, and compose functions to build more complex behavior.
Example:

```javascript
Copy code
const numbers = [1, 2, 3];
const doubledNumbers = numbers.map(num => num * 2); // Using map as a higher-order function
```

5. Declarative Code
Functional programming encourages a declarative approach, where you describe what you want to do, not how to do it. This leads to clearer, more concise code.

Best Practice: Use higher-level functions (map, filter, reduce) to express operations on collections rather than using loops or manual iterations.
Example:
javascript

Copy code

```
const numbers = [1, 2, 3, 4];
const evenNumbers = numbers.filter(num => num % 2 ===
0); // Declarative, avoids manual iteration
```

6. Function Composition

Function composition is the process of combining simple functions to create more complex ones. This leads to reusable and modular code.

Best Practice: Compose small, reusable functions to build more complex behavior, instead of writing large monolithic functions.

Example:

javascript
Copy code

```
const add2 = x => x + 2;
const multiplyBy3 = x => x * 3;
const add2AndMultiplyBy3 = x =>
multiplyBy3(add2(x));
console.log(add2AndMultiplyBy3(5)); // Output: 21
```

7. Avoiding Side Effects

In functional programming, side effects—such as modifying global variables, changing object properties, or interacting with external systems—are minimized. This makes functions easier to test, debug, and reason about.

Best Practice: Keep functions free of side effects by avoiding direct changes to external states and focusing on returning values instead.

Example:
javascript
Copy code
const add = (a, b) => a + b; // Pure, no side effects

8. Lazy Evaluation
Lazy evaluation means deferring the evaluation of an expression until its value is needed. This can optimize performance by avoiding unnecessary calculations.

Best Practice: Use lazy evaluation when working with large data sets or expensive computations. JavaScript doesn't support lazy evaluation natively, but libraries like Lodash or Ramda can help implement it.

Example:

javascript

Copy code

```
const range = (start, end) => {
    const result = [];
    for (let i = start; i <= end; i++) {
        result.push(i);
    }
    return result;
};
console.log(range(1, 1000).filter(n => n % 2 === 0)); // Lazy evaluation of the filter
```

9. Currying

Currying is a technique where a function is broken down into a sequence of functions that each take one argument. It helps in creating more specialized versions of a function by fixing some arguments.

Best Practice: Use currying to create reusable and modular functions that can be partially applied.

Example:

javascript

Copy code
```
const multiply = a => b => a * b;
const multiplyBy2 = multiply(2);
console.log(multiplyBy2(5)); // Output: 10
```

Conclusion

By adhering to functional principles such as immutability, pure functions, first-class and higher-order functions, and avoiding side effects, JavaScript developers can write more modular, maintainable, and predictable code. The use of declarative approaches, function composition, and currying also enhances code readability and reusability, enabling the creation of scalable applications that are easier to test and debug.

Avoiding Side Effects

In functional programming, avoiding side effects is a core principle that helps make code more predictable, easier to understand, and easier to test. A side effect is any observable change in the state of the application that occurs outside the scope of a function. This can include things like modifying global variables, changing the properties of objects, writing to the console, or interacting with external systems (e.g., making API calls, manipulating the DOM).

1. What Are Side Effects?

Side effects occur when a function does something beyond simply returning a value based on its inputs. These actions can change the program's state or interact with the outside world, making the function harder to reason about and test.

Common examples of side effects:

Modifying external variables:
javascript
Copy code
let count = 0;

function increment() {
    count++; // Modifies the external variable 'count'
}

Modifying objects or arrays in place:

javascript
Copy code

```javascript
const user = { name: "Alice", age: 25 };

function updateUser() {
    user.age = 26;  // Modifies the 'user' object
}
```

Writing to the console:
javascript
Copy code

```javascript
function logMessage() {
    console.log("Hello, world!");  // This is a side effect
}
```

Interacting with external systems (e.g., making API calls):
javascript
Copy code

```javascript
function fetchData() {
    fetch('https://api.example.com').then(response =>
response.json());  // External system interaction
}
```

2. Why Avoid Side Effects?

There are several reasons why functional programming encourages minimizing side effects:

a. Predictability and Consistency

Functions with no side effects always produce the same result given the same inputs, making them easier to reason about and debug.
Without side effects, you don't have to worry about changes happening in one part of the code unexpectedly affecting other parts.

b. Testability

Pure functions (those without side effects) are easier to test. Since they don't alter external state, you only need to test their inputs and outputs, without worrying about setup or teardown of external variables or states.

Example:
javascript
Copy code
// Pure function
const add = (a, b) => a + b;

console.log(add(2, 3)); // Output: 5

In contrast, a function with side effects may require you to test the system's state changes as well, complicating the test cases.

c. Concurrency and Parallelism

Functions without side effects can be executed concurrently or in parallel without worrying about race conditions or state conflicts. This is important for optimizing performance in modern applications that require high scalability.
Pure functions can be memoized (cached) because the result depends only on their inputs.

3. How to Avoid Side Effects in JavaScript

Avoiding side effects often involves writing functions that are pure—functions that rely only on their arguments to produce a result and do not alter any external state.

a. Use Immutable Data Structures

Instead of modifying objects or arrays in place, create new copies of the data with the desired modifications.

Example using the spread operator:

javascript

Copy code

```
const user = { name: "Alice", age: 25 };
const updatedUser = { ...user, age: 26 };  // Creates a new object, leaving the original unchanged
```

.b. Avoid Modifying Global State

Avoid functions that change global variables or properties of external objects. Rely on function arguments and return values instead of modifying external state.

Example:

javascript

Copy code

```
let count = 0;

// Bad: modifies global state
function increment() {
    count++;
}
```

```javascript
// Good: returns a new value
function incrementCount(count) {
    return count + 1;
}
```

c. Prefer Return Values Over Side Effects

Instead of writing to the console or modifying external variables, make your functions return values that can be used elsewhere.

Example:

javascript

Copy code

```javascript
// Side-effecting function
function updateUI(message) {
    console.log(message);  // Writes to the console (side effect)
}


// Pure function
function createMessage(name) {
    return `Hello, ${name}!`;
}
```

d. Minimize I/O Operations

While interacting with external systems (e.g., API calls or file systems) is often necessary, try to encapsulate side-effecting code in smaller, isolated functions and minimize its impact on the rest of the application.

Example: Isolate I/O functions and use them sparingly, keeping them separate from pure computation-heavy code.

javascript
Copy code

```javascript
// Side effect
function fetchData(url) {
    return fetch(url).then(response => response.json());
}

// Pure computation
function computeData(data) {
    return data.filter(item => item.active);
}
```

4. Examples of Pure vs. Impure Functions
Pure Function:

A pure function does not alter any state or produce side effects. It only returns a value based on its input.

javascript

Copy code

```javascript
const add = (a, b) => a + b; // No side effects, always returns the same output for the same inputs
```

Impure Function:

An impure function has side effects, like modifying a global variable or performing an I/O operation.

javascript

Copy code

```javascript
let total = 0;

function addToTotal(amount) {
    total += amount; // Modifies a global variable, side effect
}
```

5. Advantages of Avoiding Side Effects

Predictability: Functions with no side effects are deterministic, meaning they produce the same result for the same input every time.

Reusability: Pure functions are easier to reuse since they don't rely on or alter the external state.

Easier Debugging: With fewer side effects, it's easier to trace errors to their source and isolate problems.

Concurrency Support: Side-effect-free functions allow safe concurrent and parallel execution, making your application more performant.

6. Conclusion

Avoiding side effects is a core principle of functional programming that leads to more maintainable, testable, and predictable code. By ensuring that functions do not modify external state, relying on immutability, and avoiding side-effecting operations like I/O in non-UI code, you can write cleaner and more scalable JavaScript applications.

Writing Pure Functions

A pure function is a function that:

Always produces the same output for the same input.

Has no side effects, meaning it does not alter any external state, variables, or objects, and does not rely on or change external data.

Pure functions are a foundational concept in functional programming because they lead to more predictable, testable, and maintainable code. In JavaScript, writing pure functions is crucial for creating reliable applications and improving performance by enabling optimization techniques like memoization.

1. Characteristics of Pure Functions

A pure function has the following characteristics:

Deterministic: For the same set of input values, a pure function will always return the same result.

No Side Effects: A pure function does not modify any external state or variables, and it doesn't produce observable side effects such as logging to the console, writing to a file, or interacting with external APIs.

2. Benefits of Pure Functions

Predictability: Since pure functions always return the same output for the same inputs, they are easier to reason about and understand.

Testability: Pure functions are easier to test because they do not depend on external state or variables. You can easily test them by providing input and verifying the output.

Debugging: With no side effects and no dependencies on external state, debugging pure functions is straightforward.

Reusability: Pure functions can be reused anywhere in your application since they don't rely on or alter external state.

Concurrency: Pure functions are naturally thread-safe because they don't modify shared state, making them ideal for parallel execution in multithreaded environments.

3. How to Write Pure Functions in JavaScript

a. Avoid External State or Side Effects

A pure function must not modify any external variables, objects, or arrays. It should only depend on the input passed to it.

Example of a pure function:

javascript
Copy code

```javascript
// Pure function
const add = (a, b) => a + b;  // It only depends on the arguments and returns a value
```

Example of an impure function that modifies an external variable:

javascript
Copy code

```javascript
let total = 0;

// Impure function
function addToTotal(amount) {
    total += amount;  // Modifies the external variable 'total'
}
```

b. Do Not Modify Input Arguments

Functions should not modify their input arguments. Instead, they should create new values based on the inputs and return them.

Example of a pure function:

javascript
Copy code
```
// Pure function that returns a new value without
changing the original data
const updateUserAge = (user, newAge) => ({ ...user,
age: newAge });

const user = { name: 'Alice', age: 30 };
const updatedUser = updateUserAge(user, 31); // The
original user object is not modified
console.log(user); // { name: 'Alice', age: 30 }
console.log(updatedUser); // { name: 'Alice', age: 31 }
```

Example of an impure function that modifies the input:

javascript
Copy code
```
// Impure function that modifies the input object
const updateUserAgeImpure = (user, newAge) => {
    user.age = newAge;  // Modifies the original object
    return user;
};
```

```javascript
const user = { name: 'Alice', age: 30 };
const updatedUser = updateUserAgeImpure(user, 31);
// The original 'user' object is modified
console.log(user); // { name: 'Alice', age: 31 }
console.log(updatedUser); // { name: 'Alice', age: 31 }
```

c. Avoid Using External State or Variables

Pure functions do not rely on or modify external states, such as global variables, database states, or any data stored outside the function.

Example of a pure function:

javascript
Copy code
```javascript
const multiply = (a, b) => a * b;  // No reliance on external state
```

Example of an impure function that depends on an external variable:

javascript
Copy code

```javascript
let multiplier = 2;

// Impure function that depends on the external
variable 'multiplier'
const multiplyWithMultiplier = (a) => a * multiplier;
```

d. Return Values Instead of Side Effects

A pure function should return a value rather than performing any side effect, like modifying global variables, printing to the console, or performing I/O operations.

Example of a pure function:

javascript
Copy code
```javascript
// Pure function that returns the sum of the
arguments
const sum = (a, b) => a + b;
```
Example of an impure function that performs a side effect (writing to the console):

javascript
Copy code

```javascript
// Impure function that logs the result instead of
returning it
const logSum = (a, b) => {
  console.log(a + b); // This is a side effect
};
```

4. Examples of Pure vs. Impure Functions

Pure Function Example:

javascript

Copy code

```javascript
// Pure function that computes the square of a number
const square = (num) => num * num;

console.log(square(4)); // Output: 16
console.log(square(4)); // Output: 16 (Always the same
result for the same input)
```

Impure Function Example:

javascript

Copy code

```javascript
let result = 0;

function addToResult(num) {
```

```javascript
    result += num; // Modifies external variable 'result',
which is a side effect
    return result;
}
```

```javascript
console.log(addToResult(4)); // Output: 4
console.log(addToResult(3)); // Output: 7 (State has
changed due to previous call)
```

5. Refactoring Impure Functions to Pure Functions
Refactoring impure functions into pure functions involves:

Removing reliance on external variables.
Returning new values instead of modifying existing ones.
Example: Refactoring an Impure Function
Impure function:

javascript
Copy code
```javascript
let currentBalance = 100;

function withdraw(amount) {
    currentBalance -= amount;   // Modifies external
variable
```

```
    return currentBalance;
}
```
Refactored to pure function:

```javascript
Copy code
function withdraw(balance, amount) {
    return balance - amount;  // Returns a new value based on inputs
}

const initialBalance = 100;
const newBalance = withdraw(initialBalance, 50);
console.log(newBalance); // Output: 50 (Does not modify 'initialBalance')
```

6. Testing Pure Functions

Pure functions are easier to test because they don't depend on external states or side effects. You can test them by simply passing input values and verifying the return values.

Example test for a pure function:

javascript
Copy code
const add = (a, b) => a + b;

console.log(add(2, 3)); // Expected output: 5
console.log(add(-1, 1)); // Expected output: 0

7. Conclusion

Writing pure functions in JavaScript leads to cleaner, more maintainable, and more predictable code. By ensuring that functions are deterministic and free of side effects, developers can write applications that are easier to test, debug, and optimize. In addition, pure functions enable better performance through techniques like memoization and allow safe parallel execution, making them an essential tool in functional programming.

Embracing Immutability

Immutability is a core concept in functional programming, and it plays a pivotal role in writing clean, predictable, and maintainable code. In the context of programming, immutability refers to the idea that once a data structure is created, it cannot be changed or modified. Instead of altering existing data, new copies of the data are created with the changes applied. This concept helps avoid unintended side effects, making programs easier to reason about, debug, and test.

1. What is Immutability?

An immutable object or variable is one whose state cannot be modified after it has been created. Any operation that seems to modify the object or variable actually creates a new one with the desired change.

For example, if we have an object representing a user:

```javascript
Copy code
const user = { name: 'Alice', age: 30 };
```

An immutable approach would involve creating a new user object if we need to modify any property:

javascript
Copy code
const updatedUser = { ...user, age: 31 }; // A new object
is created with the updated age

In this case, the original user object remains unchanged, and the modification creates a new object, which adheres to the principle of immutability.

2. Benefits of Immutability

a. Predictability and Debugging
Immutability makes the program's behavior more predictable. Since data cannot be changed after its creation, you can be certain that any variable or object will not unexpectedly change during the execution of the program. This makes it easier to track down bugs and inconsistencies, as data flows in a more controlled and predictable manner.

b. No Side Effects

In an immutable system, side effects are minimized. Since objects and arrays cannot be modified directly, developers do not need to worry about unintended changes in different parts of the program. This leads to fewer bugs and easier maintenance.

c. Simplified Concurrency and Parallelism

Immutability ensures that data is not shared or altered by multiple processes at the same time. This eliminates race conditions and other issues associated with mutable data in multi-threaded or parallel environments. Immutability makes concurrency simpler and safer.

d. Easier Testing

Because immutable data cannot be modified, it is much easier to test functions. You don't need to worry about the state of the data changing in unexpected ways across different parts of the program. Testing becomes more straightforward as functions can be isolated, and their outputs are predictable based on their inputs.

3. How to Embrace Immutability in JavaScript

a. Use const to Declare Variables

In JavaScript, the const keyword ensures that a variable cannot be reassigned. While const does not make the object or array itself immutable (it only prevents reassignment), it enforces the idea that a variable should not be changed, which is a step toward immutability.

javascript
Copy code
const person = { name: 'Bob', age: 25 };
person = { name: 'Alice', age: 30 }; // Error: reassignment is not allowed

b. Avoid Direct Mutation

Instead of directly modifying an object or array, create a new copy of the data and modify that copy. In JavaScript, this can be done using methods like Object.assign(), the spread operator (...), or methods like map(), filter(), and reduce() for arrays.

For objects:
javascript
Copy code
const person = { name: 'Bob', age: 25 };

```javascript
const updatedPerson = { ...person, age: 26 }; // A new
object is created
```
For arrays:

javascript
Copy code

```javascript
const numbers = [1, 2, 3, 4];
const updatedNumbers = [...numbers, 5]; // A new
array is created
```

c. Immutable Data Structures

There are libraries available that offer immutable data structures, such as Immutable.js. These libraries provide specialized methods to manage data immutably, ensuring that operations on data return new structures rather than modifying the original.

javascript
Copy code

```javascript
const { Map } = require('immutable');
const person = Map({ name: 'Alice', age: 30 });
const updatedPerson = person.set('age', 31); // Creates
a new Map, original is unchanged
```

d. Immutable State Management

In modern JavaScript applications (especially those using React), state management is often done immutably. When using state management libraries like Redux, it is essential to ensure that the state is never mutated directly. Instead, a new state object is returned with each action.

```javascript
Copy code
const initialState = { count: 0 };

function reducer(state = initialState, action) {
    switch (action.type) {
      case 'INCREMENT':
          return { ...state, count: state.count + 1 }; // A new state object is returned
      default:
          return state;
  }
}
```

4. Common Immutable Operations in JavaScript

a. Array Operations

map(): Returns a new array with the results of calling a provided function on every element in the array.

filter(): Returns a new array containing elements that pass the condition specified in the function.

reduce(): Accumulates the array's elements into a single result without modifying the original array.

Example:

```javascript
Copy code
const numbers = [1, 2, 3];
const doubledNumbers = numbers.map(num => num * 2); // [2, 4, 6]
```

b. Object Operations

Spread operator (...): Creates a new object with properties from the original object, allowing you to modify or add properties.

Object.assign(): Copies values from one or more source objects to a target object, returning a new object.

Example:

```javascript
Copy code
const user = { name: 'Alice', age: 30 };
const updatedUser = { ...user, age: 31 }; // Returns a new object
```

5. Working with Immutable Data in Complex Applications

In larger applications, where data is often nested or more complex, immutability can become challenging to manage manually. Using specialized libraries or frameworks that enforce immutability can be beneficial for ensuring that updates to state or data structures are handled correctly and efficiently.

6. Challenges of Immutability

While immutability offers numerous advantages, it can also present challenges:

Performance: Creating new objects or arrays every time you modify data can be less efficient in terms of memory and processing, especially in large applications with complex data structures.

Verbosity: Writing immutable code can sometimes be more verbose, as you need to create copies of data instead of simply modifying the original.

However, the benefits of immutability—predictability, fewer side effects, and easier maintenance—typically outweigh the drawbacks in most functional programming scenarios.

7. Conclusion

Embracing immutability in JavaScript leads to more robust, maintainable, and testable code. By ensuring that data remains unchanged after its creation, you avoid side effects and bugs, making your applications more predictable and easier to reason about. Whether through simple object manipulation or leveraging immutable data structures, immutability is an essential concept in functional programming that helps developers write cleaner and more reliable JavaScript code.

Using Composition over Inheritance

In software development, especially when designing applications, a common principle is to favor composition over inheritance. This approach can make code more flexible, modular, and easier to maintain. While inheritance is a way to structure classes in a hierarchy (often creating tightly coupled and rigid structures), composition focuses on building complex objects by combining simpler, smaller parts, or behaviors.

1. Understanding Inheritance

Inheritance is a common feature in object-oriented programming (OOP) where classes derive properties and methods from a parent (or "super") class. This concept works well for situations with a clear hierarchical structure, such as "is-a" relationships. For example, a Dog class can inherit from an Animal class because a dog is a type of animal:

javascript
Copy code
```javascript
class Animal {
```

```
  eat() {
    console.log("Eating...");
  }
}


class Dog extends Animal {
  bark() {
    console.log("Barking...");
  }
}
```

However, as the hierarchy deepens or the application grows more complex, inheritance can lead to tightly coupled classes, making it difficult to modify or extend behavior without impacting other parts of the code. This can lead to issues like the "fragile base class" problem, where changes in a parent class can break child classes in unexpected ways.

2. What is Composition?

Composition, on the other hand, assembles objects with various, reusable behaviors. Instead of extending a class, composition involves creating objects with specific properties or functions and combining them to achieve the desired functionality. With composition, an object "has-a" behavior or characteristic rather than "is-a" certain type, allowing greater flexibility and reusability.

For example, consider a Dog that needs to bark and eat. Using composition, we can create separate objects for each behavior and combine them:

```javascript
Copy code
const eater = {
  eat() {
    console.log("Eating...");
  }
};

const barker = {
  bark() {
    console.log("Barking...");
  }
};

function createDog() {
  return Object.assign({}, eater, barker);
}
```

```
const dog = createDog();
dog.eat(); // Eating...
dog.bark(); // Barking...
```

In this example, the createDog function composes a new dog by combining the eater and barker behaviors. If we need other animals or entities that also bark or eat, we can easily reuse these behavior objects without rewriting or extending classes.

3. Advantages of Composition Over Inheritance

a. Greater Flexibility and Reusability

With composition, individual behaviors are isolated and modular. You can mix and match behaviors to create new objects, making it easier to extend functionality without impacting existing code. This approach enhances code reuse and adaptability.

b. Avoids Deep Hierarchies

Inheritance often leads to deep class hierarchies that are difficult to navigate and maintain. Composition allows you to avoid these hierarchies, reducing the risk of fragile base classes and making your code more adaptable to change.

c. Easier to Test and Debug

Because behaviors in a compositional model are more self-contained, it's easier to write tests for each behavior in isolation. Inheritance-based structures often require setting up entire class hierarchies to test a single function, which can make testing cumbersome.

d. Better Alignment with the Single Responsibility Principle (SRP)
Composition encourages the division of responsibilities across distinct behaviors, making it easier to follow SRP. Each behavior can handle a single responsibility, leading to cleaner and more modular code.

4. Implementing Composition in JavaScript

JavaScript's nature as a prototype-based language makes composition particularly easy to implement. There are several techniques for using composition, but two popular methods are mixins and higher-order functions.

a. Using Mixins

A mixin is a pattern that lets you add properties or methods from one object to another. By creating mixin objects, you can selectively "mix" behaviors into other objects.

```javascript
Copy code
const swimmer = {
  swim() {
    console.log("Swimming...");
  }
};

const flyer = {
  fly() {
    console.log("Flying...");
  }
};

function createFlyingFish() {
  return Object.assign({}, swimmer, flyer);
}

const flyingFish = createFlyingFish();
```

flyingFish.swim(); // Swimming...
flyingFish.fly(); // Flying...

Here, we define swimmer and flyer mixins, which can be combined to create a flyingFish. This allows for the creation of flexible, behavior-based entities without establishing class hierarchies.

b. Using Higher-Order Functions

Higher-order functions (HOFs) take functions as arguments or return them as results. They can also be used to add behavior to objects in a compositional manner. This approach works well when behaviors are more dynamic or need additional parameters.

```javascript
Copy code
const withSwim = (obj) => ({
  ...obj,
  swim() {
    console.log("Swimming...");
  }
});
```

```
const withFly = (obj) => ({
  ...obj,
  fly() {
    console.log("Flying...");
  }
});

const flyingFish = withFly(withSwim({}));
flyingFish.swim(); // Swimming...
flyingFish.fly();  // Flying...
```

In this example, withSwim and withFly are HOFs that return new objects with the desired behaviors. This approach is more functional and allows for flexible composition of behaviors.

5. Use Cases for Composition Over Inheritance

UI Components: Compositional design is common in UI frameworks like React, where components are built from smaller, reusable components rather than relying on class hierarchies.

Data Processing Pipelines: When working with data processing tasks, it's often useful to compose behaviors that transform or validate data, making it easier to chain operations.

Complex Entities with Varied Behaviors: Composition is ideal for situations where objects require varied or changeable behaviors, such as gaming entities with multiple abilities or service objects with specific actions.

6. Challenges of Composition

While composition has significant benefits, there are also some challenges:

Overhead in Object Creation: Creating multiple behavior objects can add memory and processing overhead. It's essential to strike a balance based on the complexity of your application.

Coordination of Behaviors: Managing interactions between different behaviors can become complex, especially if behaviors need to interact or depend on each other.

Understanding Compositional Structures: For teams accustomed to traditional inheritance, composition-based designs can be unfamiliar. This requires a shift in thinking, especially when designing object interactions.

7. Conclusion

Composition over inheritance allows JavaScript developers to build flexible, reusable, and maintainable applications. By focusing on combining small, single-responsibility behaviors instead of creating complex hierarchies, composition encourages modular code that's easy to test and modify. Embracing composition helps reduce dependencies between components, making your codebase more resilient to change and future-proof. While composition may not replace inheritance in all situations, it is a powerful tool that can improve the design and scalability of your JavaScript applications.

PART II: CORE FUNCTIONAL CONCEPTS IN JAVASCRIPT

Chapter 4
Higher-order Functions

Higher-order functions (HOFs) are a core concept in JavaScript functional programming. These functions either take other functions as arguments or return functions as their result. They enable flexible and reusable code by allowing us to treat functions as values that can be passed around and manipulated.

1. Examples of Built-in Higher-Order Functions

JavaScript includes several built-in HOFs for working with arrays, such as:

.map() – transforms each element in an array based on a function and returns a new array.
.filter() – creates a new array with elements that meet a certain condition.
.reduce() – accumulates values in an array into a single result based on a function.

javascript
Copy code

```javascript
const numbers = [1, 2, 3, 4, 5];
const doubled = numbers.map(num => num * 2); // [2, 4, 6, 8, 10]
const evens = numbers.filter(num => num % 2 === 0); // [2, 4]
const sum = numbers.reduce((acc, num) => acc + num, 0); // 15
```

2. Benefits of Higher-Order Functions

Code Reusability: HOFs allow you to apply the same function across different contexts, making your code more modular.

Flexibility: They make it easy to customize behavior, as you can pass in different functions to tailor operations without changing the core logic.

Abstraction: HOFs help encapsulate complex logic, making your code more readable and maintainable.

3. Creating Custom Higher-Order Functions

You can create custom HOFs to add specific behaviors or transformations. For example, a multiplyBy function that returns a function to multiply a number by a given factor:

javascript
Copy code
```
function multiplyBy(factor) {
   return function(num) {
      return num * factor;
   };
}

const triple = multiplyBy(3);
console.log(triple(5)); // 15
```

Higher-order functions are a powerful feature in JavaScript's functional programming, enabling clear, reusable, and scalable code by leveraging functions as first-class citizens.

What Are Higher-order Functions?

Higher-order functions (HOFs) are functions that either take other functions as arguments or return functions as their result. This is possible because JavaScript treats functions as "first-class citizens," meaning they can be assigned to variables, passed as arguments, and returned from other functions. Higher-order functions are a core concept in functional programming and enable more flexible, reusable, and concise code.

Key Features of Higher-Order Functions

Taking Functions as Arguments: HOFs can accept functions as parameters, allowing you to inject behavior or logic dynamically. For instance, JavaScript's .map(), .filter(), and .reduce() array methods are examples of higher-order functions because they accept a callback function to customize their behavior.

javascript
Copy code
```
const numbers = [1, 2, 3, 4];
const doubled = numbers.map(num => num * 2); // [2, 4, 6, 8]
```

Returning Functions: HOFs can also return a function, allowing you to create functions with specific behaviors dynamically. This is commonly used for creating functions that "remember" specific values or configurations.

```javascript
Copy code
function greet(greeting) {
  return function(name) {
    return `${greeting}, ${name}!`;
  };
}

const sayHello = greet("Hello");
console.log(sayHello("Alice")); // "Hello, Alice!"
```

Benefits of Higher-Order Functions

Reusability: They make code modular, as functions can be reused in different contexts by passing them into HOFs. Abstraction: HOFs allow you to encapsulate and abstract away repetitive logic, making code cleaner and easier to read. Customization: HOFs let you pass in different functions to tailor operations to your needs without changing the main function.

Common Examples in JavaScript

.map() – Applies a function to each element of an array and returns a new array.

.filter() – Filters elements in an array based on a condition defined in a function.

.reduce() – Reduces an array to a single value based on an accumulating function.

Higher-order functions are essential tools in JavaScript, making functional programming techniques accessible and providing flexibility to build more expressive and maintainable code.

Common Higher-order Functions (map, filter, reduce)

JavaScript includes several built-in higher-order functions for working with arrays, with three of the most commonly used being map, filter, and reduce. Each of these methods enables powerful data transformations and makes code more concise and expressive, especially in functional programming.

1. map()

The map() method creates a new array by applying a specified function to each element of the original array. This is ideal for transforming data without modifying the original array.

Example:

```javascript
Copy code
const numbers = [1, 2, 3, 4];
const doubled = numbers.map(num => num * 2);
console.log(doubled); // Output: [2, 4, 6, 8]
```

In this example, map() takes each number in the numbers array, doubles it, and returns a new array with the doubled values. The original array remains unchanged.

Use Cases:

Modifying each element in an array, like converting values from one unit to another.

Extracting specific properties from an array of objects (e.g., mapping over an array of users to get their names).

2. filter()

The filter() method creates a new array with all elements that satisfy a specified condition, as defined by a callback function. If the condition is met, the element is included in the new array; if not, it's excluded.

Example:

```javascript
Copy code
const numbers = [1, 2, 3, 4, 5];
const evens = numbers.filter(num => num % 2 === 0);
console.log(evens); // Output: [2, 4]
```

Here, filter() selects only the even numbers from the numbers array, resulting in a new array that contains [2, 4].

Use Cases:

Filtering data based on a condition, such as finding active users or valid inputs.
Removing specific elements from an array, such as filtering out negative numbers or empty strings.

3. reduce()

The reduce() method reduces an array to a single value by applying a function that accumulates each element. The method takes two parameters: the callback function and an optional initial accumulator value. The callback function is executed for each element, combining it with an accumulated result.

Example:

javascript
Copy code
```javascript
const numbers = [1, 2, 3, 4, 5];
const sum = numbers.reduce((accumulator, currentValue) => accumulator + currentValue, 0);
console.log(sum); // Output: 15
```

In this example, reduce() calculates the sum of all elements in the numbers array by adding each number to an initial accumulator value of 0. The final accumulated result is 15.

Use Cases:

Summing or accumulating values, such as calculating totals.
Transforming arrays into different data structures, like counting occurrences of elements or grouping data.
Summary of Key Differences
map() is used for transforming each item in an array and returns a new array of the same length.
filter() is used for selecting elements that match a condition, resulting in a potentially shorter array.
reduce() is used to "reduce" an array to a single value, ideal for aggregation or summarization tasks.

These higher-order functions are fundamental in JavaScript and encourage a functional approach to data manipulation, making code more modular, readable, and maintainable.

Using Higher-order Functions in JavaScript

Higher-order functions (HOFs) are an essential part of JavaScript that allow developers to write more modular, expressive, and maintainable code. HOFs, which either take functions as arguments or return functions as their output, enable a functional approach to programming that emphasizes immutability, code reuse, and flexibility.

Why Use Higher-Order Functions?

Higher-order functions provide several benefits in JavaScript programming:

Reusability: HOFs allow code to be more reusable by accepting different functions for different behaviors.
Modularity: They promote modularity by helping break down complex logic into smaller, composable functions.
Readability: Using HOFs can make code more readable and concise, especially for operations like transformations and filtering of data.

Key Higher-Order Functions in JavaScript

map(): Transforms each element in an array according to a provided function and returns a new array with the transformed values.

javascript
Copy code
```
const numbers = [1, 2, 3, 4];
const squared = numbers.map(num => num * num);
console.log(squared); // Output: [1, 4, 9, 16]
```

Here, map() applies a squaring function to each number, creating a new array with the results.
filter(): Filters elements in an array based on a condition and returns a new array with only the elements that meet the criteria.

javascript
Copy code
```
const ages = [15, 25, 18, 30];
const adults = ages.filter(age => age >= 18);
console.log(adults); // Output: [25, 18, 30]
```

filter() selects only the elements that satisfy the condition, creating a new array with the filtered values.

reduce(): Reduces an array to a single value by accumulating values according to a provided function.

javascript
Copy code
```
const numbers = [1, 2, 3, 4];
const sum = numbers.reduce((total, num) => total + num, 0);
console.log(sum); // Output: 10
```

reduce() accumulates each element in the array, calculating the sum here and returning a single value.

forEach(): Iterates over each element in an array, allowing operations to be applied without returning a new array.

javascript
Copy code
```
const names = ['Alice', 'Bob', 'Charlie'];
names.forEach(name => console.log(`Hello, ${name}!`));
```

forEach() is ideal for applying side effects, like logging or updating external variables, without modifying the original array.

Advanced Higher-Order Functions

In addition to the basics, JavaScript lets you create custom HOFs, enabling you to add specific behaviors or encapsulate logic within functions:

Function Returning Function: Creating functions that return other functions to "remember" a certain value or configuration.

```javascript
Copy code
function multiplyBy(factor) {
  return function(num) {
    return num * factor;
  };
}

const double = multiplyBy(2);
console.log(double(5)); // Output: 10
```

Here, multiplyBy is a higher-order function that returns a new function based on a specific factor, creating customized functions like double.

Composing Functions: Combining functions together to create more complex behaviors from simple, reusable functions.

javascript
Copy code
```
const add = a => b => a + b;
const multiply = a => b => a * b;

const addThenMultiply = (a, b, c) => multiply(add(a)(b))(c);
console.log(addThenMultiply(2, 3, 4)); // Output: 20
```
Using HOFs to combine add and multiply in this way lets you build more flexible and readable operations.

Practical Applications

Data Processing: Filtering, mapping, and reducing are common in processing data collections, like filtering active users, mapping product prices, or summarizing sales totals.

Event Handling: In web development, HOFs are used in functions like addEventListener to manage dynamic behavior.

Asynchronous Operations: Functions like then() in JavaScript Promises enable chaining and modularizing asynchronous code, which is a hallmark of functional-style coding.

Conclusion

Higher-order functions in JavaScript enable a functional programming style that is both powerful and expressive. By leveraging HOFs like map, filter, reduce, and creating custom functions, developers can write more concise, modular, and flexible code, transforming complex logic into manageable, reusable operations.

Chapter 5

Closures and Lexical Scoping

Closures are a fundamental concept in JavaScript that allow a function to "remember" the scope in which it was created, even when it's executed outside of that scope. When a function is defined within another function, it captures and retains access to variables from its outer function's scope. This captured environment is called a closure.

Lexical Scoping refers to the way JavaScript determines variable scope based on the structure of the code. In a lexically scoped language like JavaScript, functions access variables based on where they are physically written in the code, not where they are called from.

How Closures Work

A closure occurs when an inner function references variables from its outer function, and this reference is preserved even after the outer function has finished executing.

Example:

```javascript
Copy code
function outer() {
  let count = 0;
  return function inner() {
    count++;
    return count;
  };
}

const counter = outer();
console.log(counter()); // Output: 1
console.log(counter()); // Output: 2
```

In this example, inner is a closure that "remembers" the count variable from outer, allowing it to increment and retain the value even after outer has completed.

Benefits of Closures

Data Privacy: Closures can create private variables that can't be accessed directly from outside functions.

Stateful Functions: They allow functions to "remember" and modify state, enabling persistent data within functions.

Encapsulation: Closures help encapsulate behavior and state, making code more modular and maintainable.

Closures and lexical scoping are powerful tools in JavaScript, enabling encapsulation, data privacy, and more advanced functional programming techniques.

Understanding Closures in JavaScript

Closures are a powerful and unique feature in JavaScript that allow a function to access variables from its lexical scope, even after the outer function has completed execution. Essentially, closures let a function "remember" the environment in which it was created.

How Closures Work

Closures are created when a function is defined within another function and references variables from its outer function. Even after the outer function finishes executing, the inner function retains access to these variables, effectively "closing over" the lexical scope.

Example of a Closure
javascript
Copy code

```javascript
function outerFunction() {
    let counter = 0;
    return function innerFunction() {
        counter++;
        return counter;
    };
}

const increment = outerFunction();
console.log(increment()); // Output: 1
console.log(increment()); // Output: 2
```

In this example:

outerFunction defines a local variable counter and returns innerFunction.

innerFunction is a closure because it captures counter from the scope of outerFunction.

Each time increment is called, innerFunction "remembers" and modifies counter, even though outerFunction has completed execution.

Benefits and Use Cases of Closures

Data Privacy: Closures enable private variables, as data in a closure cannot be accessed directly from outside the function.

```javascript
Copy code
function secretMessage() {
    const message = "This is private!";
    return function reveal() {
        return message;
    };
}

const revealSecret = secretMessage();
```

console.log(revealSecret());   //   Output: "This   is   private!"

Maintaining State: Closures allow functions to retain state, making them useful for situations where you need to "remember" information across function calls.

Callback Functions: Closures are commonly used in asynchronous code, such as event handlers or callbacks, where functions retain access to variables after the outer function has executed.

Partial Application and Currying: Closures are useful in functional programming patterns like currying, where a function is broken down into multiple functions that each take one argument.

Key Points

Lexical Scope: Closures work due to JavaScript's lexical scoping, where functions "remember" variables from the scope in which they were defined.
Memory Management: Closures keep references to outer scope variables, so be mindful of memory usage, as improperly used closures can lead to memory leaks.

Closures are a foundational concept in JavaScript, making them crucial for mastering advanced programming techniques, creating modular code, and handling asynchronous tasks.

Practical Applications of Closures

Closures are incredibly versatile in JavaScript and have numerous practical applications, especially for managing state, creating encapsulated functionality, and handling asynchronous programming. Here are some of the most common use cases:

1. Data Privacy and Encapsulation

Closures allow you to create private variables, as data captured within a closure cannot be accessed directly from outside the function. This is useful for creating encapsulated modules and private state within objects.

Example: Creating Private Variables

javascript
Copy code

```javascript
function createCounter() {
    let count = 0; // private variable
    return function() {
        count++;
        return count;
    };
}

const counter = createCounter();
console.log(counter()); // Output: 1
console.log(counter()); // Output: 2
```

In this example, the count variable is private to the createCounter function. Each call to counter() increments and returns the count without exposing it directly.

2. Function Factories

Closures can be used to create functions with preset configurations or "factory functions." This technique enables the generation of specific functions based on parameters provided to the outer function.

Example: Custom Greeting Generator

```javascript
Copy code
function greetingGenerator(greeting) {
  return function(name) {
    return `${greeting}, ${name}!`;
  };
}

const sayHello = greetingGenerator("Hello");
console.log(sayHello("Alice")); // Output: "Hello, Alice!"
```

Here, greetingGenerator creates new greeting functions like sayHello with a preset greeting message. This can be applied to create a variety of functions with unique configurations, like customized loggers or formatters.

3. Event Handlers and Callbacks

Closures are often used in event handlers and asynchronous functions to "capture" variables from their creation scope. This ensures that the callback or event handler has access to the variables even when executed later.

Example: Using Closures in Event Handlers

```javascript
Copy code
function setupButtonClick(buttonId, message) {

document.getElementById(buttonId).addEventListener('click', function() {
    console.log(message);
  });
}

setupButtonClick("myButton", "Button clicked!");
```

In this example, the callback function retains access to the message variable, even though setupButtonClick has completed execution. This enables the button click handler to log the correct message each time.

4. Partial Application and Currying

Closures make it easy to implement partial application and currying, which are functional programming techniques that allow functions to be applied gradually by fixing some arguments and returning a new function for the remaining arguments.

Example: Partial Application

javascript
Copy code
```javascript
function multiply(a) {
  return function(b) {
    return a * b;
  };
}

const double = multiply(2);
console.log(double(5)); // Output: 10
```

In this example, multiply(2) creates a new function that doubles any input, using closures to "remember" the value of a.

5. Memoization and Caching

Closures can be used to implement memoization, which is a caching technique to store computed results for expensive function calls and reuse them when the same inputs occur again.

Example: Memoization of a Function

javascript
Copy code
```javascript
function memoizedFactorial() {
    const cache = {};
    return function factorial(n) {
        if (n in cache) return cache[n];
        if (n === 0 || n === 1) return 1;
        cache[n] = n * factorial(n - 1);
        return cache[n];
    };
}
```

```javascript
const factorial = memoizedFactorial();
console.log(factorial(5)); // Output: 120
console.log(factorial(5));  // Output: 120 (retrieved from cache)
```

In this example, memoizedFactorial creates a closure with a cache object to store the computed factorials, avoiding redundant calculations.

6. State Management in Functional Components (e.g., React)

In functional programming contexts like React, closures are frequently used to manage state and create hooks. Closures allow functions to "remember" and modify values without requiring classes or object instances.

Example: Custom Counter Hook in React

javascript
Copy code

```javascript
function useCounter(initialValue) {
    let count = initialValue;
    return [
        () => count,          // Getter
          () => { count++; return count; }  // Increment function
    ];
}
```

```javascript
const [getCount, increment] = useCounter(0);
console.log(getCount()); // Output: 0
console.log(increment()); // Output: 1
```

In this example, useCounter is a simple custom hook that uses closures to store and modify a count variable, demonstrating how closures can maintain state in functional programming.

7. Iterators and Generators

Closures help in implementing iterators and custom generator functions, as they can hold and update state each time they are called.

Example: Creating an Iterator with Closures

```javascript
Copy code
function createRangeIterator(start, end) {
    let current = start;
    return function() {
        if (current <= end) {
            return current++;
        } else {
```

```
    return null; // end of range
  }
};
}
```

```
const next = createRangeIterator(1, 3);
console.log(next()); // Output: 1
console.log(next()); // Output: 2
console.log(next()); // Output: 3
console.log(next()); // Output: null
```

In this example, createRangeIterator returns an iterator function that "remembers" the current value of current, incrementing it with each call.

Conclusion

Closures provide a flexible way to maintain data, manage state, and create private functionality in JavaScript. With closures, JavaScript developers can achieve data encapsulation, function factories, event handling, memoization, and more, enabling powerful solutions for complex application needs.

Scope and Lexical Binding

Scope and lexical binding are fundamental concepts in JavaScript that determine how variables are accessed and managed in code. Understanding these concepts is key to avoiding unexpected behavior and writing effective, predictable code.

Scope in JavaScript

Scope defines the accessibility of variables and functions. JavaScript has two main types of scope:

Global Scope: Variables declared outside any function or block are in the global scope. They can be accessed from anywhere in the program.

javascript
Copy code
let globalVar = "I'm global!";

```javascript
function logGlobal() {
    console.log(globalVar); // Accessible
}

logGlobal(); // Output: "I'm global!"
```

Local Scope: Variables declared within a function or block (using let or const) are only accessible within that function or block.

```javascript
Copy code
function localScope() {
    let localVar = "I'm local!";
    console.log(localVar); // Accessible
}

console.log(localVar); // Error: localVar is not defined
```

Block Scope: With let and const, JavaScript supports block scope, meaning variables declared in a block (like an if statement or loop) are limited to that block.

javascript

Copy code
```
if (true) {
    let blockVar = "I'm block-scoped!";
}
console.log(blockVar); // Error: blockVar is not defined
```

Lexical Binding

Lexical binding, also known as lexical scoping, is a rule that determines how variable names are resolved based on where they are declared in the code. In JavaScript, a function's scope is fixed at the time of its creation, not at the time it is called. This means that a function will always look for variables in its original scope, regardless of where it's invoked later.

How Lexical Binding Works

When a function is defined, it captures the scope where it was created. This is known as the lexical environment, and it includes all the variables that were in scope at the time of the function's definition. This captured environment enables the function to retain access to these variables even if it's called outside that scope.

Example of Lexical Binding in JavaScript

javascript
Copy code

```javascript
function outer() {
  const outerVar = "Outer scope";

  function inner() {
    console.log(outerVar); // "Outer scope"
  }

  return inner;
}

const innerFunc = outer();
innerFunc(); // Output: "Outer scope"
```

In this example, inner captures the outerVar variable from outer's scope. When innerFunc is called later, it still has access to outerVar due to lexical binding, even though outer has finished executing.

Why Lexical Binding Matters

Closures: Lexical binding is the basis for closures, which allow functions to access and remember variables from their outer scopes.

Predictability: Lexical scoping ensures consistent behavior, as functions always reference the scope where they were defined, regardless of where they are called.

Data Privacy: By using closures and lexical binding, functions can maintain private variables, allowing data to be kept out of the global scope.

Lexical Binding and Arrow Functions

Arrow functions in JavaScript follow lexical binding for their this keyword as well. Unlike regular functions, arrow functions don't have their own this; they inherit it from their lexical scope, which can make them particularly useful for callbacks and methods.

Example: Lexical Binding with Arrow Functions

```javascript
Copy code
function Person(name) {
  this.name = name;
  this.greet = () => {
    console.log(`Hello, my name is ${this.name}`);
  };
```

```
}
```

const person = new Person("Alice");
person.greet(); // Output: "Hello, my name is Alice"

Here, the arrow function greet inherits the this context from Person, making it simpler to use in cases where the this context needs to be retained.

Conclusion

Scope and lexical binding allow for organized code, variable control, and predictable behavior. Understanding these concepts helps in writing functions that behave as expected, capturing the right context and avoiding common issues such as variable shadowing and incorrect this references.

Chapter 6
Recursion in Functional Programming

Recursion is a key technique in functional programming where a function calls itself to solve a problem in smaller, manageable parts. Instead of relying on loops (like for or while), recursion breaks down a problem into smaller subproblems, with each recursive call processing a subset until reaching a base case—a condition that stops further recursion.

How Recursion Works

A recursive function generally has two parts:

Base Case: Defines when the recursion should stop, usually when the input has been reduced to a minimal level.
Recursive Case: The function calls itself with a modified argument to progress towards the base case.
Example: Calculating Factorial Recursively

```javascript
Copy code
function factorial(n) {
    if (n <= 1) return 1; // Base case
```

```
    return n * factorial(n - 1);  // Recursive case
}
console.log(factorial(5));  // Output: 120
```

In this example, factorial(5) calls itself with decreasing values of n until it reaches the base case (n <= 1), at which point recursion stops and the results are multiplied back up.

Advantages in Functional Programming

Recursion is favored in functional programming due to its stateless and pure function properties, which align well with the functional paradigm. Recursion helps eliminate mutable state and iterative loops, making code easier to reason about and often more elegant. Additionally, functions like map, filter, and reduce often use recursion implicitly to process collections.

Tail Recursion Optimization

Languages that support tail-call optimization (TCO) can handle certain types of recursion more efficiently by reusing stack frames, making recursive functions perform as efficiently as loops. Although JavaScript does not fully optimize tail calls in all engines, tail recursion is common in functional programming to help manage stack usage.

Basics of Recursion

Recursion is a programming technique where a function calls itself in order to solve a problem. This approach is especially useful for tasks that can be divided into similar sub-tasks, such as navigating hierarchical data structures (e.g., trees) or performing calculations like factorials and Fibonacci sequences.

How Recursion Works

A recursive function must have two essential parts:

Base Case: This is the condition that stops the recursion. Without a base case, the function would keep calling itself indefinitely, leading to a stack overflow error.

Recursive Case: This is where the function calls itself with modified arguments to move closer to the base case with each call.

Example: Simple Recursive Function (Factorial)

```javascript
Copy code
function factorial(n) {
    if (n <= 1) return 1;  // Base case
    return n * factorial(n - 1);  // Recursive case
}
console.log(factorial(5));  // Output: 120
```

In this example:

The base case is n <= 1, which stops recursion and returns 1.
The recursive case is n * factorial(n - 1), where the function calls itself with n - 1 until it reaches the base case.
How Recursion Solves Problems
Recursion is particularly effective when:

Problems can be broken into smaller instances of the same problem.
Iterative solutions are less natural or more complex.

For example, calculating the Fibonacci sequence, finding files in nested folders, and working with tree-like structures (e.g., DOM trees or organization charts) are commonly solved with recursion.

Example: Recursive Fibonacci Function

javascript
Copy code

```javascript
function fibonacci(n) {
   if (n <= 1) return n; // Base case
      return fibonacci(n - 1) + fibonacci(n - 2); // Recursive case
}
console.log(fibonacci(5)); // Output: 5
```

Advantages and Disadvantages of Recursion

Advantages:

Elegance: Recursive solutions are often more concise and easier to understand, especially for complex problems.

Alignment with Functional Programming: Recursion is often used in functional programming, where functions avoid mutable state and loops.

Disadvantages:

Performance: Recursive functions can be slower and use more memory than iterative solutions, especially for deep recursion levels.
Stack Overflow: Without a proper base case, recursion can lead to a stack overflow error.

Tail Recursion

In some languages, tail recursion optimization (TCO) helps reduce memory usage by reusing the same stack frame for recursive calls that are in the "tail" position, meaning they are the last operation in the function. JavaScript has limited TCO support, so recursive functions should be used carefully in situations with many nested calls.

Conclusion

Recursion is a powerful tool for breaking down complex problems and structuring code in a clear, hierarchical manner. By using a well-defined base case and recursive logic, recursion allows problems to be solved naturally and concisely, although efficiency and potential stack limitations should be considered.

Implementing Recursive Functions in JavaScript

Recursive functions in JavaScript are functions that call themselves until they reach a base case. This approach is especially useful for solving problems that involve repetitive tasks or data structures that naturally form a hierarchy, such as arrays, trees, or nested objects.

Key Elements of a Recursive Function

Base Case: The condition that stops the recursion. Without it, the function would continue calling itself indefinitely, resulting in a stack overflow error.

Recursive Case: The part of the function where it calls itself with updated parameters, progressing toward the base case in each call.

Example 1: Factorial of a Number
A common example of recursion is the calculation of the factorial of a number. In a factorial calculation, n! is equal to n * (n-1) * (n-2) * ... * 1, which naturally fits a recursive approach.

javascript
Copy code
```javascript
function factorial(n) {
    if (n <= 1) return 1; // Base case: when n is 1 or 0, return 1
    return n * factorial(n - 1); // Recursive case: multiply n by factorial(n-1)
}

console.log(factorial(5)); // Output: 120
```

Here:

The base case is when n <= 1, at which point recursion stops.

The recursive case calls factorial(n - 1) until it reaches the base case.

Example 2: Calculating Fibonacci Sequence

The Fibonacci sequence is another classic example, where each term is the sum of the two preceding terms: $F(n) = F(n - 1) + F(n - 2)$.

javascript
Copy code

```javascript
function fibonacci(n) {
    if (n <= 1) return n; // Base cases: return n if 0 or 1
        return fibonacci(n - 1) + fibonacci(n - 2); // Recursive case
}

console.log(fibonacci(5)); // Output: 5
```

In this function:

The base case is n <= 1, where it returns n.

The recursive case calls fibonacci(n - 1) and fibonacci(n - 2) to sum the preceding terms.

Note: While elegant, this implementation is inefficient for larger values of n due to repeated calculations. Optimizing with memoization or using an iterative approach is often preferable for performance.

Example 3: Summing an Array with Recursion
Recursion can also be used to iterate through arrays, adding each element until all elements are summed up.

```javascript
Copy code
function sumArray(arr) {
    if (arr.length === 0) return 0; // Base case: empty array returns 0
    return arr[0] + sumArray(arr.slice(1)); // Recursive case: add first element to sum of rest
}

console.log(sumArray([1, 2, 3, 4, 5])); // Output: 15
```

In this function:

The base case is an empty array, which returns 0.

The recursive case adds arr[0] to the result of sumArray(arr.slice(1)).

Practical Use Case: Traversing Nested Data Structures
Recursion is particularly useful for traversing tree-like or nested data structures, such as file systems or JSON objects with nested arrays.

```javascript
Copy code
function findValue(obj, key) {
    if (key in obj) return obj[key]; // Base case: return the value if key is found

  for (let k in obj) {
      if (typeof obj[k] === 'object') { // If nested object, call recursively
          const result = findValue(obj[k], key);
              if (result !== undefined) return result; // Return if found
      }
  }
    return undefined; // Return undefined if key is not found
```

```
}
```

```
const data = { a: 1, b: { c: 2, d: { e: 3 } } };
console.log(findValue(data, 'e')); // Output: 3
```

In this example, findValue searches for a key in a nested object. The recursion stops when the key is found, or the entire structure has been traversed.

Tail Recursion Optimization

Some programming languages support tail recursion optimization (TCO), where recursive calls in the tail position (i.e., the last operation in the function) can be optimized to avoid increasing the call stack. While JavaScript does not fully support TCO in all engines, tail recursion is a useful practice for certain functional patterns.

javascript
Copy code
```
function factorialTail(n, accumulator = 1) {
    if (n <= 1) return accumulator; // Base case with accumulated result
        return factorialTail(n - 1, n * accumulator); //
Tail-recursive call
```

```
}
```

console.log(factorialTail(5)); // Output: 120

Tips for Writing Recursive Functions

Define the Base Case: Ensure the base case is well-defined and reachable to prevent infinite recursion.

Progress Toward the Base Case: Each recursive call should modify arguments or data, so the function approaches the base case.

Consider Performance: For complex calculations, consider memoization or iterative solutions to improve efficiency.

Conclusion

Recursive functions in JavaScript offer elegant solutions to complex problems, especially those involving hierarchical or nested structures. By carefully structuring base and recursive cases, recursion becomes a powerful tool for building scalable, maintainable code.

Tail Call Optimization

Tail Call Optimization (TCO) is an optimization technique that helps reduce the memory overhead of recursive function calls. When a function calls itself recursively, each call typically adds a new stack frame to the call stack, consuming memory. TCO reduces this stack usage by reusing the current function's stack frame for tail-recursive calls, rather than creating a new one. This allows recursive functions to run as efficiently as loops, avoiding stack overflow errors and improving performance.

What Is a Tail Call?

A tail call is a function call that is the final action in another function. This means there are no further operations after the recursive call returns, allowing the current function to pass control directly to the next call without needing to retain information about the current stack frame.

Example of a Tail Call:

```javascript
Copy code
function factorialTail(n, accumulator = 1) {
    if (n <= 1) return accumulator; // Base case with
accumulated result
    return factorialTail(n - 1, n * accumulator); //
Tail-recursive call
}
console.log(factorialTail(5)); // Output: 120
```

In factorialTail, the recursive call factorialTail(n - 1, n *
accumulator) is the last operation in the function, making it
a tail call. If the JavaScript engine supports TCO, it will
reuse the current stack frame for each recursive call,
minimizing memory usage.

Why TCO Matters

For functions that call themselves many times (e.g.,
traversing a deep data structure or computing large
Fibonacci numbers), TCO can significantly improve
efficiency. Without TCO, deeply recursive calls could lead to

a stack overflow error, as each recursive call adds to the call stack until it reaches its memory limit.

With TCO:

The function can run with constant stack space, no matter the recursion depth.
Recursive functions can handle large inputs as efficiently as loops.
This optimization is particularly useful in functional programming, where recursion is often preferred over iteration.

How TCO Works

In a TCO-enabled environment, when the compiler or interpreter detects a tail call, it:

Replaces the current stack frame with the next one, effectively "recycling" the memory allocated for the function call.
Avoids growing the stack, allowing the function to operate without adding new frames.
TCO is common in languages optimized for functional programming, like Scheme, but is not fully supported in all

JavaScript environments. While the ECMAScript 6 (ES6) specification includes TCO, not all JavaScript engines have implemented it, and as of now, it is not reliably available across all platforms.

Writing Tail-Recursive Functions

To make a function tail-recursive:

Ensure that the recursive call is the last operation in the function.
Use accumulators to pass along intermediate results. This way, the function doesn't need to perform further operations after the recursive call.

Example: Calculating Sum with Tail Recursion

```javascript
Copy code
function sumTail(arr, accumulator = 0) {
    if (arr.length === 0) return accumulator; // Base case with accumulated result
    return sumTail(arr.slice(1), accumulator + arr[0]); // Tail-recursive call
}
```

console.log(sumTail([1, 2, 3, 4, 5])); // Output: 15

In this example:

The recursive call sumTail(arr.slice(1), accumulator + arr[0]) is the last action.
The accumulator keeps track of the ongoing sum, allowing the function to return directly.

Limitations of TCO in JavaScript

While TCO is included in the ECMAScript specification, its actual implementation in JavaScript engines (such as V8, SpiderMonkey, or JavaScriptCore) varies. Many popular JavaScript environments, including those in most browsers, do not fully support TCO, meaning tail-recursive functions may still cause stack overflow with deep recursion.

When to Use TCO

If you are working in a JavaScript environment that supports TCO (e.g., some configurations of Node.js), tail-recursive functions can be a powerful tool. For other cases:

Consider Iteration: Use an iterative solution if recursion depth is a concern.
Memoization: Cache results for complex recursive functions to avoid redundant calls.

Conclusion

Tail Call Optimization (TCO) can make recursive functions as memory-efficient as loops by reusing stack frames in recursive calls. While TCO is defined in the ECMAScript specification, support varies across JavaScript environments, so it's important to understand your runtime's capabilities. By writing functions to be tail-recursive, you can take advantage of TCO where available, resulting in more efficient, memory-friendly code.

Avoiding Common Pitfalls in Recursion

Recursion is a powerful tool in programming, especially in functional programming. However, it requires careful implementation to avoid pitfalls that can lead to inefficient code, errors, or unexpected results. Here are some common issues and tips on how to avoid them when working with recursion in JavaScript.

1. Missing or Incorrect Base Case

The base case is the condition that stops the recursion. If you don't have a base case, or if the base case is incorrect, your function will recurse indefinitely, leading to a stack overflow error.

Solution: Always define a clear base case that the function will eventually reach. Carefully check that the base case is achievable with each recursive call.

Example:

javascript
Copy code
```
function countdown(n) {
    if (n <= 0) return; // Base case
    console.log(n);
    countdown(n - 1); // Recursive call
}

countdown(5); // Outputs: 5, 4, 3, 2, 1
```

2. Infinite Recursion

Infinite recursion occurs when the recursive calls don't approach the base case, causing the function to call itself endlessly. This often results from incorrectly modifying the parameters in each call.

Solution: Make sure each recursive call progresses toward the base case by appropriately modifying the parameters. Validate that the function parameters are moving in the correct direction to eventually meet the base case.

Example:

javascript
Copy code
```javascript
function sumToN(n, sum = 0) {
   if (n <= 0) return sum; // Base case
      return  sumToN(n - 1, sum + n); // Progressing towards base case
}

console.log(sumToN(5)); // Output: 15
```

3. Deep Recursion and Stack Overflow

When recursion depth is too great (e.g., in deeply nested data structures), it can lead to a stack overflow as each recursive call consumes stack memory. JavaScript does not fully support tail call optimization in most environments, which means deep recursion may cause memory issues.

Solution:

For large inputs, consider using an iterative approach or rewriting the function in a way that avoids deep recursion.
If recursion is necessary, you may also explore memoization to cache results and reduce redundant calculations,

especially in recursive functions with overlapping subproblems (e.g., Fibonacci calculations).

Example (Memoization for Fibonacci):

javascript
Copy code

```
const fibMemo = (n, memo = {}) => {
  if (n <= 1) return n;
  if (memo[n]) return memo[n];
  memo[n] = fibMemo(n - 1, memo) + fibMemo(n - 2, memo);
  return memo[n];
};

console.log(fibMemo(50)); // Output: 12586269025 (without deep recursion)
```

4. Excessive Memory Usage

Recursive functions that handle large datasets or involve multiple calls (e.g., tree traversal) can consume a lot of memory, especially if new arrays or objects are created in each call.

Solution:

Avoid creating new objects or arrays in each call unless necessary.

For array-based recursion, consider using slicing carefully or in-place modifications if the function doesn't require immutability.

Example:

javascript
Copy code

```javascript
function sumArray(arr, index = 0) {
    if (index >= arr.length) return 0; // Base case
    return arr[index] + sumArray(arr, index + 1); // Progressing toward base case
}

console.log(sumArray([1, 2, 3, 4, 5])); // Output: 15
```

5. Overlapping Subproblems

Some recursive algorithms, like calculating Fibonacci numbers, end up recalculating the same values repeatedly.

This redundant work can make the function very slow for larger inputs.

Solution: Use memoization to store already calculated results and avoid recalculating them. Memoization is particularly useful for dynamic programming problems, like Fibonacci or other divide-and-conquer algorithms.

Example (Memoization in Factorial):

javascript
Copy code
```javascript
const factorialMemo = (n, memo = {}) => {
    if (n <= 1) return 1;
    if (memo[n]) return memo[n];
    memo[n] = n * factorialMemo(n - 1, memo);
    return memo[n];
};
```

console.log(factorialMemo(10)); // Output: 3628800

6. Unintended Side Effects

Recursion should ideally be free from side effects. Side effects occur when the function changes something outside of its own scope, like modifying a global variable or altering an argument in each recursive call. This can lead to unpredictable behavior and make debugging difficult.

Solution: Write pure functions for recursion whenever possible, meaning the function only depends on its arguments and doesn't alter external variables or data. Use accumulators or pass modified data as function arguments to avoid side effects.

Example of a Pure Recursive Function:

javascript
Copy code
```javascript
function reverseString(str, reversed = '') {
    if (str.length === 0) return reversed; // Base case
    return reverseString(str.slice(1), str[0] + reversed); //
Tail-recursive call
}

console.log(reverseString("hello")); // Output: "olleh"
```

7. Not Tail-Optimizing Where Possible

JavaScript engines don't universally support tail call optimization (TCO), but writing tail-recursive functions can make your code ready for TCO in supported environments. Tail-recursive functions avoid adding new stack frames, which helps reduce memory usage.

Solution: Use tail recursion by ensuring that the recursive call is the last operation in the function, allowing potential TCO by the JavaScript engine.

Example (Tail Recursion with Accumulator):

```javascript
Copy code
function factorialTail(n, accumulator = 1) {
    if (n <= 1) return accumulator; // Base case with accumulated result
    return factorialTail(n - 1, n * accumulator); // Tail-recursive call
}

console.log(factorialTail(5)); // Output: 120
```

Conclusion

Recursion in JavaScript is a powerful but nuanced tool. Avoiding common pitfalls requires attention to base cases, memory usage, and side effects. By structuring recursive functions carefully, considering alternatives like memoization and tail recursion, and understanding the limitations of recursion in JavaScript, you can create efficient, reliable recursive functions that work well across various scenarios.

PART III: ADVANCED FUNCTIONAL TECHNIQUES

Chapter 7
Function Composition

Function composition is the process of combining multiple functions to create a single function that performs a series of operations in sequence. In functional programming, it allows for the building of complex functionality from smaller, simpler functions, improving code modularity and readability.

How It Works
When functions are composed, the output of one function becomes the input for the next. For example, if you have two functions, f and g, composing them $(f(g(x)))$ means g runs first, and its output is passed to f.

Example in JavaScript

In JavaScript, you can manually compose functions, or use libraries like Lodash or Ramda for composition utilities.

javascript
Copy code

```
const add = x => x + 2;
const multiply = x => x * 3;

const addThenMultiply = x => multiply(add(x));

console.log(addThenMultiply(4)); // Output: 18
```

Benefits

Modularity: Breaking down complex tasks into smaller, reusable functions.

Readability: Enhances code clarity by reducing nested calls.

Testability: Each function can be tested in isolation, making debugging easier.

Function composition helps in creating cleaner, more maintainable code, especially in functional programming approaches.

What Is Function Composition?

Function composition is a fundamental concept in functional programming that involves combining two or more functions to produce a new function. In a composed function, each function in the sequence receives the output of the previous function as its input, creating a chain of transformations. This approach helps make code more modular, readable, and reusable by enabling complex operations to be broken down into simpler steps.

How It Works

In mathematical terms, if you have two functions, $f(x)$ and $g(x)$, the composition of these functions is represented as $f(g(x))$. In this composition:

$g(x)$ is applied first.
The result of $g(x)$ is then passed to $f(x)$ as its input.
In programming, function composition often applies functions from right to left (e.g., $f(g(x))$), but many

functional programming libraries also allow left-to-right composition (e.g., g(f(x))).

Example in JavaScript
In JavaScript, you can compose functions to create a more complex function that performs multiple steps sequentially. Here's an example:

javascript
Copy code
```
const addTwo = x => x + 2;
const square = x => x * x;

const addAndSquare = x => square(addTwo(x));

console.log(addAndSquare(3)); // Output: 25
```

In this example:

addTwo is applied to 3, giving 5.
The result, 5, is passed to square, giving 25.

Benefits of Function Composition

Modularity: Composing functions allows developers to break down complex tasks into smaller, reusable pieces, which can be combined as needed.

Readability: It makes code cleaner and more understandable by separating each operation.

Testability: Each function in a composition can be tested independently, making it easier to debug and maintain code.

Function Composition Libraries

Libraries like Lodash and Ramda offer utilities to simplify function composition. For example, Ramda's compose function allows you to create complex functions by composing other functions from right to left.

```javascript
Copy code
import { compose } from 'ramda';

const addTwo = x => x + 2;
const square = x => x * x;

const addAndSquare = compose(square, addTwo);
```

console.log(addAndSquare(3)); // Output: 25

Conclusion

Function composition is a powerful technique for building flexible, maintainable code. It enables developers to reuse smaller functions and combine them in different ways to solve complex problems. By promoting modularity and readability, function composition is a core principle in functional programming and a valuable tool in JavaScript development.

Composing Functions in JavaScript

Composing functions in JavaScript involves combining multiple functions into a single, cohesive function. This practice is a core principle of functional programming, making it easier to build modular, readable, and reusable code. By creating compositions, you can pass the output of

169

one function directly as the input to another, streamlining operations and enhancing code organization.

How Function Composition Works

In function composition, multiple functions are chained together in a specific order. If you have two functions, f(x) and g(x), composing them as f(g(x)) means that g(x) runs first, and its result is then passed as an argument to f(x). This chaining allows for complex operations to be constructed from smaller, single-purpose functions.

Manual Composition Example

Without any libraries, you can manually compose functions by nesting them:

```javascript
Copy code
const toUpperCase = str => str.toUpperCase();
const addExclamation = str => str + '!';

const shout = str => addExclamation(toUpperCase(str));
```

console.log(shout("hello")); // Output: "HELLO!"

In this example:

toUpperCase converts the string to uppercase.
The result is passed to addExclamation, which appends an exclamation mark.

Using a Composition Utility Function

You can create a compose function to simplify chaining:

javascript
Copy code
const compose = (...fns) => x => fns.reduceRight((acc, fn) => fn(acc), x);

const shout = compose(addExclamation, toUpperCase);
console.log(shout("hello")); // Output: "HELLO!"

In this compose function:

reduceRight applies functions from right to left, starting with the input x and passing the result through each function in sequence.

Functional Programming Libraries for Composition

Libraries like Ramda and Lodash provide compose and flow functions to streamline composition. Ramda.compose composes functions from right to left, while lodash.flow composes from left to right. Using these libraries can make compositions cleaner and more expressive, especially when chaining multiple functions.

javascript
Copy code
```javascript
import { compose } from 'ramda';

const shout = compose(addExclamation, toUpperCase);
console.log(shout("hello")); // Output: "HELLO!"
```

Benefits of Composing Functions in JavaScript

Modularity: Functions can be kept simple and single-purpose, then composed to handle complex logic.

Reusability: Smaller, reusable functions can be composed in different ways for various tasks.

Readability: Composition enhances readability by reducing deeply nested calls and allowing complex transformations to be expressed in a sequence.

Example with Real-world Functions

Composing functions is especially useful in data processing, such as transforming an array of values:

```javascript
Copy code
const double = x => x * 2;
const increment = x => x + 1;
const sumArray = arr => arr.reduce((acc, x) => acc + x, 0);

const processArray = compose(sumArray, arr => arr.map(double), arr => arr.map(increment));

console.log(processArray([1, 2, 3])); // Output: 18
```

In this example:

Each element in the array is incremented.

Each incremented value is then doubled.

The array values are summed up, providing a final result of 18.

Conclusion

Composing functions in JavaScript enables a more functional approach to building applications. By combining small, pure functions, developers can create more structured and maintainable code. With the help of libraries or manual composition, function composition becomes an effective way to handle complex operations and promote code readability and reuse.

Using compose and pipe Functions

In functional programming, compose and pipe are higher-order functions used to combine multiple functions into a single function. They allow you to pass data through a series of transformations, enhancing readability, reusability, and modularity. The primary difference between compose and pipe is the order in which they apply functions.

What is compose?

compose applies functions from right to left. If you have functions f, g, and h, the composition compose(f, g, h)(x) will evaluate as f(g(h(x))). This is similar to how functions are nested, where the innermost function is evaluated first.

```javascript
Copy code
const toUpperCase = str => str.toUpperCase();
const exclaim = str => str + '!';
const greet = str => `Hello, ${str}`;

const welcome = compose(greet, exclaim, toUpperCase);
```

console.log(welcome("world")); // Output: "Hello, WORLD!"

In this example:

toUpperCase is applied to "world", producing "WORLD".
exclaim appends "!", resulting in "WORLD!".
greet adds "Hello, ", giving the final output "Hello, WORLD!".
What is pipe?
pipe is essentially the opposite of compose, applying functions from left to right. This makes pipe useful when you want to read the function chain in the same order as it's executed. If you have f, g, and h, then pipe(f, g, h)(x) evaluates as h(g(f(x))).

Using the same example as above, pipe would look like this:

javascript
Copy code
const welcome = pipe(toUpperCase, exclaim, greet);

console.log(welcome("world")); // Output: "Hello, WORLD!"

In this example:

toUpperCase is applied to "world".

exclaim adds the exclamation mark.

greet forms the greeting, yielding "Hello, WORLD!".

Choosing Between compose and pipe

Order of Operations: Use compose if you prefer reading functions from right to left, and pipe if you prefer left-to-right.

Readability: pipe often feels more natural for reading data flows since it aligns with the sequence of transformations.

Library Support: Libraries like Ramda and Lodash provide both compose and pipe, enabling you to choose based on preference or use case.

Examples of Practical Use Cases

Data Transformation Pipelines: When processing arrays or objects, compose and pipe let you combine transformations cleanly.

javascript

```
Copy code
const double = x => x * 2;
const increment = x => x + 1;
const square = x => x * x;

const processNumber = pipe(increment, double,
square);

console.log(processNumber(3)); // Output: 64
```

Data Parsing and Formatting: In scenarios where data goes through various cleaning and formatting functions, pipe and compose help manage the flow.

```javascript
Copy code
const trim = str => str.trim();
const toLowerCase = str => str.toLowerCase();
const addPeriod = str => str + '.';

const formatText = compose(addPeriod, toLowerCase,
trim);

console.log(formatText("    HELLO WORLD    ")); //
Output: "hello world."
```

Implementation of compose and pipe

If not using a library, you can implement simple versions of compose and pipe:

javascript
Copy code
```
const compose = (...fns) => x => fns.reduceRight((acc, fn) => fn(acc), x);
const pipe = (...fns) => x => fns.reduce((acc, fn) => fn(acc), x);
```
compose: Applies functions from right to left using reduceRight.
pipe: Applies functions from left to right using reduce.

Summary

compose: Combines functions from right to left, similar to nesting.
pipe: Chains functions from left to right, making the order of execution more intuitive.

Both compose and pipe allow for creating clear and readable data transformation pipelines, essential in functional programming.

Choosing between them often depends on readability preferences, but both help make code modular and expressive by chaining together simple, single-purpose functions.

Chapter 8
Currying and Partial Application

Currying and partial application are techniques in functional programming that transform functions to increase reusability, flexibility, and composability.

Currying

Currying transforms a function with multiple arguments into a series of functions, each taking a single argument. Instead of passing all arguments at once, currying allows you to pass them one at a time. This enables more modular code and can simplify function chaining.

For example, a standard function for adding two numbers might look like this:

```javascript
Copy code
const add = (a, b) => a + b;
console.log(add(2, 3)); // Output: 5
```

Curried, it becomes:

javascript
Copy code
```javascript
const add = a => b => a + b;
console.log(add(2)(3)); // Output: 5
```

Here, add(2) returns a function that waits for the next argument, b.

Partial Application

Partial application is similar but slightly different: it allows you to fix a few arguments of a function in advance, creating a new function with fewer arguments. This is useful when certain values remain constant across many function calls.

For example:

javascript
Copy code
```javascript
const multiply = (a, b) => a * b;
const double = multiply.bind(null, 2);

console.log(double(5)); // Output: 10
```

Here, double is a partially applied version of multiply with the first argument set to 2.

Key Differences

Currying: Breaks down a function into nested, single-argument functions.
Partial Application: Fixes some arguments of a function to create a new, more specific function.

Benefits
Both techniques enable function reusability and modularity. Currying and partial application are widely used in functional programming to simplify code, make it more adaptable, and allow chaining and composition.

Introduction to Currying

Currying is a functional programming technique in which a function that takes multiple arguments is transformed into a sequence of functions, each taking a single argument. This process allows functions to be evaluated incrementally, with each function returning another function that accepts the next argument, until all arguments are supplied.

The primary benefit of currying is that it enhances the reusability and flexibility of functions by enabling partial application and function composition. It allows for a more modular approach to coding, making it easier to build complex functionality from simple, reusable components.

How Currying Works

To understand currying, consider a function that takes two arguments, a and b, and adds them together:

javascript
Copy code
```
const add = (a, b) => a + b;
```

In its curried form, the same function would be transformed into a sequence of functions where each one takes a single argument:

javascript
Copy code
const add = a => b => a + b;

Here's how it works:

The first call to add provides the first argument (a).
The second call provides the second argument (b).
The result is the sum of a and b.

Example of Currying in Action
javascript
Copy code
const multiply = a => b => a * b;

const multiplyByTwo = multiply(2); // Creates a new
function
console.log(multiplyByTwo(5)); // Output: 10

In this example:

multiply(2) creates a new function that expects the second
argument b.

multiplyByTwo(5) calls the curried function with the second argument, producing the result 10.

Currying and Partial Application

Currying can be used in combination with partial application, where some of the arguments of a curried function are provided in advance. This allows for the creation of specialized versions of functions. For example, you can fix one argument and later provide the remaining ones:

javascript
Copy code
```javascript
const add = a => b => c => a + b + c;

const addFive = add(5);   // Partially apply the first argument
console.log(addFive(2)(3)); // Output: 10
```

Here, addFive is a partially applied version of add with the first argument (a) set to 5. It can then accept the remaining arguments.

Benefits of Currying

Reusability: Curried functions can be reused with different sets of arguments, which makes your code more modular.

Partial Application: Currying allows for easy partial application of functions, where some arguments are fixed in advance, creating specialized versions of the function.

Function Composition: Curried functions can be composed easily, enabling more declarative and readable code.

Cleaner and More Declarative Code: Currying helps make functions more declarative by breaking complex functions into simpler ones, each with a single responsibility.

Conclusion

Currying is a powerful functional programming technique that transforms a function taking multiple arguments into a series of functions that take one argument each. It allows for better code modularity, reusability, and flexibility, especially in combination with partial application. Although it can be challenging to grasp at first, currying is a valuable tool in building functional and efficient JavaScript applications.

Implementing Currying in JavaScript

Currying is a common pattern in functional programming, and JavaScript's flexible function handling makes it a perfect language for implementing and utilizing curried functions. In this section, we'll explore how to implement currying in JavaScript.

Basic Currying

At its core, currying involves transforming a function that accepts multiple arguments into a series of functions that each accept one argument. Here's a simple example of implementing currying manually:

Example 1: Basic Currying

Suppose you have a function that adds two numbers:

javascript
Copy code

const add = (a, b) => a + b;

We can convert this function into a curried version:

javascript
Copy code
const curriedAdd = a => b => a + b;

Now, instead of calling curriedAdd(2, 3), you call curriedAdd(2)(3). The first call returns a function that waits for the second argument, and then the second argument is passed in to calculate the result.

javascript
Copy code
console.log(curriedAdd(2)(3)); // Output: 5

This is how basic currying works: each function takes one argument and returns a new function that takes the next argument until all arguments are provided.

Implementing a Generic Currying Function
While writing currying manually for each function works, you can create a generic curried function that works for any

function with multiple arguments. This makes currying reusable and more convenient.

Example 2: A Generic Currying Function

Here's how you can implement a generic currying function:

```javascript
Copy code
const curry = (fn) => {
  return function curried(...args) {

    // If the number of arguments is enough to call the function
    if (args.length >= fn.length) {
      return fn(...args);
    } else {
      // Otherwise, return a function that collects more arguments
      return function(...newArgs) {
        return curried(...args, ...newArgs);
      };
    }
  };
};
```

Explanation:

fn: This is the original function that we want to curry.
curried: This function takes any number of arguments and either calls fn if enough arguments are collected or returns a new function to collect more arguments.
args.length >= fn.length: Checks if the number of arguments collected is sufficient to invoke the original function.

Example 3: Using the Generic curry Function
Now, let's use the curry function to curry any function:

javascript
Copy code
```javascript
const add = (a, b, c) => a + b + c;

const curriedAdd = curry(add);

console.log(curriedAdd(1)(2)(3)); // Output: 6
```

In this example, curriedAdd is a curried version of the add function. You can pass arguments one by one, and the result is returned once all arguments are provided.

Currying with Multiple Arguments

Currying can be useful when you have functions that take multiple arguments, and you want to break down the arguments step by step. Here's an example with a function that calculates the area of a rectangle:

javascript
Copy code
```
const area = (length, width) => length * width;
const curriedArea = curry(area);

console.log(curriedArea(5)(10)); // Output: 50
```

Handling Default Values

Currying also allows for the use of default values. When applying currying, if an argument is not provided, the function can still be executed with default values or behavior.

javascript
Copy code
```
const greet = (greeting = 'Hello', name = 'World') =>
`${greeting}, ${name}!`;
const curriedGreet = curry(greet);

console.log(curriedGreet('Hi')('Alice'));  // Output: Hi,
Alice!
console.log(curriedGreet()());  // Output: Hello, World!
```

Benefits of Currying

Modular Code: Breaking down functions into smaller, curried functions allows you to create more reusable and composable code.

Partial Application: Currying enables partial application, allowing you to fix certain parameters ahead of time and apply them later.

Cleaner Code: You can pass arguments step by step, leading to clearer and more declarative function calls.

Conclusion

Currying is a powerful functional programming technique in JavaScript that allows functions to be broken down into smaller functions that each take one argument. This modular approach helps with reusability, readability, and flexibility. Implementing currying manually or using a generic curried function helps you apply this pattern to any function in your codebase, enabling better code composition and partial application.

Benefits of Currying and Partial Application

Currying and partial application are two foundational techniques in functional programming, often used together to create more flexible, reusable, and modular code. While they share some similarities, each brings its own set of advantages. Here, we'll explore the benefits of both curried functions and partial application, highlighting how they can improve your code.

Benefits of Currying

Currying involves transforming a function that takes multiple arguments into a sequence of functions, each taking a single argument. This approach offers several key benefits:

1. Improved Code Reusability

Modular Design: By breaking down a function into smaller, single-argument functions, you can reuse those functions in different contexts with different arguments. This promotes cleaner, more modular code.

Reusable Partial Functions: You can create specialized versions of a curried function by partially applying arguments. This reduces code duplication, as you can create new functions from existing ones.

For example, a curried function can be reused in many different ways:

javascript
Copy code
```
const multiply = a => b => a * b;
```

```javascript
const multiplyByTwo = multiply(2);    // Partial application
console.log(multiplyByTwo(5)); // Output: 10
```

2. Partial Application

Flexible Argument Handling: Currying allows partial application, meaning you can "pre-load" some arguments while leaving others to be provided later. This is particularly useful in cases where certain parameters are consistent across multiple function calls.

javascript
Copy code

```javascript
const add = a => b => a + b;

const addFive = add(5);
console.log(addFive(10));  // Output: 15
```

3. Enhanced Function Composition

Composability: Curried functions can be more easily composed with other functions, allowing for greater flexibility and reusability in function chains. This leads to more declarative code and better separation of concerns.

For example:

javascript
Copy code

```javascript
const add = a => b => a + b;
const multiply = a => b => a * b;

const compose = (f, g) => x => f(g(x));

const addFiveThenDouble = compose(multiply(2), add(5));
console.log(addFiveThenDouble(10)); // Output: 30
```

4. Better Readability and Clarity

Explicit Argument Handling: With currying, it becomes clear which arguments are passed and when. This can make your code more readable and expressive, as the behavior of functions becomes more predictable.

Benefits of Partial Application

Partial application, while similar to currying, involves fixing some arguments of a function while leaving others to be applied later. It provides additional benefits, especially when working with functions that need to be customized with certain constant values.

1. Customizing Functions

Simplified Code: By fixing some parameters, you can create new specialized functions without having to repeat logic. This is particularly useful for functions that will be called with the same values repeatedly.
For example:

```javascript
Copy code
const greet = (greeting, name) => `${greeting}, ${name}!`;

const sayHello = greet.bind(null, 'Hello');  // Fix the 'greeting' argument
console.log(sayHello('Alice')); // Output: Hello, Alice!
```

2. Cleaner and More Focused Functions

Focused Functions: Partial application allows you to create functions that focus on specific aspects of behavior. By binding certain arguments ahead of time, you simplify the function's purpose and make it more adaptable.

For example, a function for logging data can be partially applied to include a standard message or log type:

javascript
Copy code
```
const log = (type, message) => console.log(`[${type}] ${message}`);
const logError = log.bind(null, 'ERROR');
logError('An unexpected error occurred.');
```

3. Reduced Repetition

Minimizing Repetition: Partial application helps you avoid repeating the same arguments across multiple calls to a function. Once you fix some arguments, you can reuse the resulting function without needing to pass those arguments every time.

javascript
Copy code

```javascript
const fetchData = (url, method, headers) => { /* Fetch data logic */ };

const get = fetchData.bind(null, 'GET');
const post = fetchData.bind(null, 'POST');

get('/api/data', { /* headers */ });
post('/api/data', { /* headers */ });
```

4. Improved Code Maintainability

Easier Modifications: Since partial application allows you to isolate and reuse common logic, modifying the behavior of functions becomes easier. If you need to change the behavior for a specific subset of arguments, you can adjust only the part of the function that is relevant.

Key Differences and Complementary Usage

While currying transforms a function to take one argument at a time, partial application fixes some of the arguments, producing a new function that requires fewer arguments. Though they can be used independently, they complement each other and are often used together to enhance the flexibility and modularity of code.

Example of Both in Action

javascript
Copy code
```
const multiply = a => b => a * b;

const multiplyByThree = multiply(3);   // Curried function
const result = multiplyByThree(5);      // Partial application
console.log(result); // Output: 15
```

In this case, the curried function multiplyByThree is a partially applied version of the multiply function, customized to always multiply by 3.

Conclusion

Both currying and partial application offer substantial benefits for writing cleaner, more reusable, and flexible code. Currying improves function composability, makes code more modular, and encourages the use of small, reusable functions. Partial application, on the other hand, allows you to fix arguments ahead of time, reducing repetition and simplifying function calls. Together, these techniques are essential tools in functional programming that can significantly enhance the design and maintainability of JavaScript applications.

Chapter 9
Functors and Monads

In functional programming, functors and monads are abstract concepts that help manage and manipulate data structures in a more composable and functional way. Both of these concepts enable you to work with data transformations in a predictable and consistent manner, but they serve different purposes and have different behaviors.

Functors

A functor is a type of container or data structure that implements a map operation, allowing you to apply a function to its contents while preserving the structure. Functors enable you to transform the values inside a container without affecting the structure itself.

Key Properties of Functors:

Identity: Applying the identity function to the functor's value should not change the value inside the functor.

Composition: Applying two functions in sequence to the functor should be equivalent to applying the composed function.

Example in JavaScript:

```javascript
Copy code
// A simple Functor: A Box that holds a value
class Box {
  constructor(value) {
    this.value = value;
  }

  // map applies a function to the value inside the Box
  map(fn) {
    return new Box(fn(this.value));  // Apply fn to the value inside
  }
}

const box = new Box(3);
const newBox = box.map(x => x * 2);  // Applies (3 * 2) = 6
console.log(newBox.value);  // Output: 6
```

In this example, map applies a function to the value inside the Box without changing the structure of the Box.

Monads

A monad is a more powerful abstraction than a functor. While functors allow you to apply functions to the values inside containers, monads provide additional capabilities for handling computations that involve chaining operations, managing side effects, or dealing with computations that may fail or be delayed.

Monads must satisfy three key properties:

Unit (or return): A way to wrap a value into a monadic context (a container).
Bind (or flatMap): A function that applies a transformation and "unwraps" the value from the container before applying the next function in the chain, returning a new monadic value.
Associativity: Operations involving monads should be associative, meaning the order of applying operations does not matter.

Example in JavaScript:

javascript
Copy code

```javascript
class Maybe {
  constructor(value) {
    this.value = value;
  }

  // "Bind" to apply a function and "unwrap" the value
  bind(fn) {
    if (this.value === null || this.value === undefined) {
      return new Maybe(null);   // If value is null/undefined, return a "Nothing" monad
    }
    return fn(this.value);
  }
}

// Usage example: Handling a computation that might fail
const safeDivide = (a, b) => b === 0 ? new Maybe(null) : new Maybe(a / b);

const result = new Maybe(10)
```

```
  .bind(value => safeDivide(value, 2))  // 10 / 2
  .bind(value => safeDivide(value, 3)); // 5 / 3

console.log(result.value);  // Output: 1.666...
```

In this example, Maybe is a monad that helps handle computations that might fail. If any of the computations return null or undefined, it prevents errors and keeps the computation chain safe.

Differences Between Functors and Monads

Map vs. Bind: A functor supports the map operation, while a monad supports the bind (or flatMap) operation, which is similar but more powerful, enabling chaining of operations.
Handling Side Effects: Monads can be used to manage side effects like state, I/O, or failures, while functors are typically used for simple transformations of values.
Unwrapping: Monads provide the mechanism to "unwrap" the value inside the container for further computations (using bind), whereas functors only map values without unwrapping.

Conclusion

Functors are useful for transforming values inside containers (like lists or Maybe types) while preserving the structure of the container.
Monads extend functors by providing additional functionality for chaining operations and handling more complex data transformations, such as managing failures or side effects.

Both concepts are essential in functional programming as they provide powerful abstractions for working with data and computations in a consistent, composable, and safe way.

Understanding Functors in JavaScript

In functional programming, a functor is a data structure that allows you to apply a function to its contained values, transforming them while keeping the original structure intact. This "mapping" of functions onto data containers makes functors highly useful for creating flexible and reusable code, especially when working with data collections or more complex data structures.

What Is a Functor?

At its core, a functor is any data structure that implements a map method, which takes a function as an argument and applies it to each element within the structure. The map method returns a new instance of the functor with the transformed values, leaving the original structure unaffected.

In JavaScript, arrays are commonly used as a basic example of a functor since they natively support the map method. This map method applies a function to each element in the array and returns a new array with the transformed values.

Basic Functor Example: Array as a Functor

The following code shows how an array functions as a functor in JavaScript:

javascript
Copy code
const numbers = [1, 2, 3];

const doubledNumbers = numbers.map(n => n * 2);
console.log(doubledNumbers); // Output: [2, 4, 6]

Here, numbers.map(n => n * 2) applies the n => n * 2 function to each element in numbers, resulting in a new array with each number doubled. The original numbers array remains unchanged, demonstrating the immutability and preservation of structure characteristic of functors.

Creating a Custom Functor

You can create your own functor by defining a data structure with a map method that applies a function to its internal value. For instance, let's create a simple Box functor that holds a single value and allows transformations through map:

```javascript
Copy code
class Box {
  constructor(value) {
    this.value = value;
  }

  map(fn) {
```

```
    return new Box(fn(this.value));    // Apply the
function and return a new Box
  }
}
```

```
const box = new Box(5);
const updatedBox = box.map(x => x + 3); // Adds 3 to
the value in the Box
console.log(updatedBox.value);  // Output: 8
```

In this example, Box acts as a functor by implementing map, which applies the provided function (x => x + 3) to the contained value (5). Instead of modifying the original box, it returns a new Box with the updated value. This is essential for immutability and functional purity.

Key Properties of Functors

Functors should follow certain properties to ensure consistency:

Identity: Applying the identity function should not alter the functor's value.

javascript

```
Copy code
const box = new Box(10);
console.log(box.map(x => x).value);  // Output: 10
```

Composition: Applying two functions in sequence should produce the same result as applying a single composed function.

```javascript
Copy code
const addTwo = x => x + 2;
const multiplyByThree = x => x * 3;
const composedFunction = x => multiplyByThree(addTwo(x));

const box = new Box(5);
const result1 = box.map(addTwo).map(multiplyByThree);  // Applies each function in sequence
const result2 = box.map(composedFunction);  //
```

Applies the composed function

```
console.log(result1.value);  // Output: 21
console.log(result2.value);  // Output: 21
```

Benefits of Functors in JavaScript

Data Transformation: Functors simplify data transformation within structures like arrays or custom containers.

Immutability: Functors promote immutability by ensuring transformations produce new instances rather than modifying the original data.

Composability: With map, functions can be composed in sequence, making transformations more modular and flexible.

Error Handling: In more complex scenarios, functors can be used to manage computations that might fail, as in Maybe or Either functors, which help prevent runtime errors by safely handling null or undefined values.

Conclusion

In JavaScript, functors provide a powerful abstraction for transforming values within data structures in an immutable and predictable way. By leveraging the map method, functors allow for consistent, reusable transformations, making your code more modular, functional, and declarative. Whether using arrays, promises, or custom containers like Box, functors play a crucial role in building flexible, composable applications.

The Concept of Monads

In functional programming, monads are a powerful abstraction used to handle operations in a predictable and composable way. They help manage computations that might involve side effects, optional values, or sequences of transformations, allowing functional code to stay clean and declarative. Monads are especially useful in managing tasks like chaining multiple operations, handling errors gracefully, and ensuring data transformations follow a structured flow.

Monad Basics

A monad is essentially a type that wraps a value and provides a way to apply functions to that value in a controlled manner. Each monad has two primary operations:

Unit (or of): A function that takes a value and wraps it in the monadic context. This initializes the monad with a value.

Bind (or flatMap / chain): A function that applies a transformation to the monadic value and returns a new monad. This is what allows chaining of operations, where each function is applied to the result of the previous computation.

Why Use Monads?

Monads provide a consistent way to handle values and transformations without the need to break the flow of functional composition. They can be thought of as "pipelines" through which data flows, with each transformation applied only if certain conditions are met, such as the presence of a value or the success of a previous step.

This is particularly helpful in:

Error handling: Managing computations that might fail, such as a network request.

Handling null/undefined values: Avoiding runtime errors by using monads like Maybe or Option, which safely handle missing values.

Asynchronous operations: Managing promises or other asynchronous flows.

Example of a Monad in JavaScript: The Maybe Monad
The Maybe monad is commonly used to handle optional values, like values that may be null or undefined. It allows chaining of operations that only execute if the value exists, preventing errors related to accessing properties or functions on null values.

javascript
Copy code
```
class Maybe {
  constructor(value) {
    this.value = value;
  }

  // Unit: Wraps a value in the monadic context
  static of(value) {
```

```
    return new Maybe(value);
  }

  // Bind: Applies a function if the value exists,
otherwise returns the original monad
  map(fn) {
    if (this.value == null) {   // Checks for null or
undefined
      return this;   // Returns the original monad if
there's no value
    }
    return Maybe.of(fn(this.value));  // Wraps the result
in a new monad
  }
}

// Usage
const result = Maybe.of(10)
  .map(x => x + 2)  // 12
  .map(x => x * 3); // 36

console.log(result.value);  // Output: 36

const nullResult = Maybe.of(null)
  .map(x => x + 2)
```

```javascript
.map(x => x * 3);
```

console.log(nullResult.value);   **// Output: null (no errors are thrown)**

In this example, the Maybe monad allows chaining functions without worrying about null checks at each step. If the initial value is null, all operations are safely bypassed, and null is returned at the end.

Key Monad Properties

Monads follow three fundamental laws that ensure consistency:

Left identity: Wrapping a value in a monad and then applying a function should be the same as applying the function directly.

javascript
Copy code
Maybe.of(value).map(f) === f(value)

Right identity: Applying of or return after a monadic operation should return the same monad.

javascript
Copy code
maybe.map(Maybe.of) === maybe

Associativity: The order of operations should not affect the final result.

javascript
Copy code
maybe.map(f).map(g) === maybe.map(x => g(f(x)))

Types of Monads

Maybe/Option: Handles missing or null values without runtime errors.

Either: Represents values that could be one of two types, often used for error handling.

Promise: Manages asynchronous computations, used widely in JavaScript.

List: Enables chaining of operations on collections.

Conclusion

Monads in JavaScript (like Promise, Maybe, or custom monads) are immensely valuable tools for structuring complex, sequential, or conditional logic. They allow for building predictable, composable, and safe workflows, which can make code clearer and reduce runtime errors. Although they can be abstract, monads ultimately provide a practical solution to managing complex data flows in functional programming.

Practical Use Cases for Functors and Monads

In functional programming, functors and monads are powerful structures for managing complex operations in a clean, composable way. While they might seem abstract at first, their practical applications can simplify common programming tasks, such as error handling, asynchronous operations, data transformations, and working with optional values. Here's an overview of how they're used in real-world JavaScript scenarios.

1. Handling Optional Values with the Maybe Monad

One of the most common use cases for the Maybe monad is handling values that might be null or undefined. This prevents errors that occur when trying to access properties or call functions on missing values.

Example: Safely accessing nested properties

```javascript
Copy code
class Maybe {
  constructor(value) {
    this.value = value;
  }

  static of(value) {
    return new Maybe(value);
  }

  map(fn) {
          return this.value  ==  null  ?  this  :
Maybe.of(fn(this.value));
  }
}
```

```
// Usage
const user = { name: 'Alice', address: { city:
'Wonderland' } };
const city = Maybe.of(user)
  .map(user => user.address)
  .map(address => address.city);

console.log(city.value); // Output: 'Wonderland'

const noCity = Maybe.of(null)
  .map(user => user.address)
  .map(address => address.city);

console.log(noCity.value);     // Output: null (safe
handling)
```

Using the Maybe monad ensures that if any property is missing along the chain, no error is thrown, and a safe null value is returned instead.

2. Managing Errors with the Either Monad

The Either monad, which typically has two forms (Left for errors and Right for success), is useful for handling computations that might fail. Instead of using try-catch blocks, Either lets you structure error-handling directly in your function chain.

Example: Validating user input

```javascript
Copy code
class Either {
  static of(value) {
    return new Right(value);
  }
}

class Right extends Either {
  constructor(value) {
    super();
    this.value = value;
  }

  map(fn) {
    return Either.of(fn(this.value));
  }
}
```

```javascript
class Left extends Either {
  constructor(value) {
    super();
    this.value = value;
  }

  map(fn) {
    return this;  // Ignore further operations on failure
  }
}

// Helper functions
const validateName = name => name ? Either.of(name)
: new Left('Name is required');
const capitalize = name => name.toUpperCase();

// Usage
const result = validateName('Alice')
  .map(capitalize);

console.log(result instanceof Right ? result.value :
result.value);  // Output: 'ALICE'

const errorResult = validateName('')
  .map(capitalize);
```

```
console.log(errorResult    instanceof    Left    ?
errorResult.value : errorResult.value);    // Output:
'Name is required'
```

In this example, Either allows safe chaining without manual error checks at each step. If validation fails, further operations are bypassed.

3. Working with Asynchronous Data Using the Promise Monad

The Promise monad is well-suited to managing asynchronous operations in JavaScript, such as data fetching. By chaining operations with then, promises allow you to handle async data without needing nested callbacks.

Example: Fetching and processing API data

javascript
Copy code
```
fetch('https://api.example.com/data')
  .then(response => response.json())
  .then(data => data.map(item => item.value))
```

```
.then(values => console.log(values))
.catch(error => console.error('Fetch error:', error));
```

Promises simplify asynchronous data flows, allowing developers to chain transformations and handle errors consistently.

4. Transforming Data with the List Functor

Functors like Array in JavaScript allow you to map over each element in a collection, applying functions and transforming data in a clean, functional way.

Example: Processing an array of numbers

javascript
Copy code
```javascript
const numbers = [1, 2, 3, 4, 5];
const doubled = numbers.map(num => num * 2);
console.log(doubled);  // Output: [2, 4, 6, 8, 10]
```

By using map, a functor method, each item is doubled without needing explicit loops, making the code concise and readable.

5. Pipelining Transformations Using Composition

Function composition is a functional approach to building pipelines of operations. Libraries like Ramda provide compose and pipe functions to help with monadic composition, chaining transformations with functions like map and chain.

Example: Data transformation pipeline

```javascript
Copy code
const R = require('ramda');

const add = x => y => x + y;
const multiply = x => y => x * y;

const transform = R.pipe(
  add(5),
  multiply(3)
);

console.log(transform(2));  // Output: 21 ((2 + 5) * 3)
```

Composition creates reusable, declarative pipelines for data transformations, essential in functional programming for keeping logic modular.

6. Safely Handling Asynchronous Errors Using Promises and Eithers

Combining the Promise monad with Either provides an effective solution for managing both asynchronous operations and potential errors within those operations.

Example: Fetching and validating data with async/await and Either

```javascript
Copy code
const fetchData = async (url) => {
  try {
    const response = await fetch(url);
    if (!response.ok) throw new Error('Network error');
    const data = await response.json();
    return Either.of(data);
  } catch (error) {
    return new Left(error.message);
  }
}
```

```
};

// Usage
fetchData('https://api.example.com/data')
  .then(result => {
    if (result instanceof Left) {
      console.error('Error:', result.value);
    } else {
      console.log('Data:', result.value);
    }
  });
```

This approach centralizes error handling without interrupting the function chain, making the code clean and error-resistant.

Conclusion

Functors and monads allow for expressive, safe, and composable handling of complex operations in JavaScript. By incorporating these concepts, developers can manage optional values, handle errors gracefully, compose data transformations, and work effectively with asynchronous data. These structures reduce error-prone code, support modular programming, and encourage functional principles that improve code maintainability and readability.

PART IV: FUNCTIONAL PATTERNS AND APPLICATIONS

Chapter 10
Error Handling in Functional Programming

In functional programming, error handling focuses on managing errors as data rather than through exceptions. This approach encourages using functional constructs like monads (e.g., Either and Maybe), which allow errors to be represented as values. Instead of interrupting the function flow, these monads enable chaining of operations, skipping or handling errors seamlessly.

For example, the Either monad can handle success (Right) and failure (Left) values. Functions can map over Right to continue operations or fall back to Left without breaking the chain. This makes error handling more predictable and keeps functions pure by avoiding side effects. This style aligns with functional programming's focus on composability and predictability, improving code readability and robustness.

Additionally, using Promises in JavaScript (a monadic structure for asynchronous code) further supports clean error handling with .catch for asynchronous flows, allowing consistent handling across sync and async code. This approach keeps functions concise, reducing the need for nested try-catch blocks.

.

Error Handling Strategies

In functional programming, error handling aims to manage failures gracefully without breaking the flow of functions. This approach emphasizes pure functions, composability, and immutability, ensuring that errors are handled in a structured way. Here are some effective error-handling strategies used in functional programming:

1. Using Monads for Error Management

Monads like Either and Maybe (or Option) are commonly used to encapsulate potential failures. Instead of throwing exceptions, these monads wrap a value in two cases:

Right/Success (when an operation is successful)
Left/Failure (when an error occurs)
These monads allow chaining operations while handling errors at the end, preventing errors from disrupting the flow.

Example in JavaScript (Either Monad):

```javascript
Copy code
const Right = x => ({
  map: f => Right(f(x)),
  fold: (f, g) => g(x)
});

const Left = x => ({
  map: f => Left(x),
  fold: (f, g) => f(x)
});

const fromNullable = x => (x != null ? Right(x) :
Left("Error: Value is null"));
```

```javascript
// Usage
const result = fromNullable("data")
  .map(value => value.toUpperCase())
  .fold(
    error => `Failed: ${error}`,
    data => `Success: ${data}`
  );
console.log(result);  // Output: "Success: DATA"
```

2. Using Promises for Asynchronous Errors

In JavaScript, Promises and async/await are monadic tools for handling asynchronous operations. They allow errors to be caught with .catch for a consistent, readable flow, which is crucial in functional code.

Example:

```javascript
javascript
Copy code
const fetchData = async (url) => {
  try {
    const response = await fetch(url);
```

```javascript
  if (!response.ok) throw new Error('Network error');
  const data = await response.json();
  return Right(data);
 } catch (error) {
  return Left(error.message);
 }
};
```

3. Using the Maybe Monad for Optional Values

The Maybe monad (often called Option in some languages) is useful when dealing with values that could be null or undefined. This allows functions to continue running even when some data is missing, without throwing errors.

javascript
Copy code
```javascript
const Maybe = value => ({
    map: fn => (value == null ? Maybe(null) : Maybe(fn(value))),
  fold: (f, g) => (value == null ? f() : g(value))
});

const result = Maybe("Hello")
  .map(str => str.toUpperCase())
```

```
.fold(
  () => "Error: Value is null",
  str => `Success: ${str}`
);
console.log(result);  // Output: "Success: HELLO"
```

4. Functional Composition with Error Handling

Functional programming allows for composition where multiple small functions are combined into one, creating a pipeline of transformations. In error handling, functions like compose or pipe can include checks for errors and propagate them down the chain without breaking.

5. Validation and Early Returns

For input validation, functional programming uses early returns or short-circuiting to stop function execution at the first encountered error. Monads can also handle these cases by returning Left when a validation fails, effectively skipping further operations.

6. Pure Functions for Predictable Error Handling

Pure functions are deterministic, meaning they will always produce the same output for the same input. When combined with immutability and statelessness, pure functions simplify error tracking, making issues more predictable and manageable.

Conclusion

These error-handling strategies in functional programming create safer, more readable, and composable code. By treating errors as data, developers can create chains of operations that gracefully handle failures, improving robustness while adhering to functional principles.

Using Either, Maybe, and Option Types

In functional programming, handling the possibility of failure, missing data, or invalid values is done through specific types that allow safer, more predictable code. Either, Maybe, and Option are data structures that represent optional or uncertain values without using exceptions or nulls. Each type helps manage common cases like error handling, optional values, or invalid states in a functional, composable way.

1. Either Type

The Either type is commonly used to represent two possible outcomes: a success and a failure. It has two "sides"—usually Right (for success) and Left (for failure). Rather than throwing exceptions, Either allows a function to return a value that can be processed differently based on success or failure.

Example: Validating user input

javascript
Copy code
```javascript
class Either {
  static right(value) {
    return new Right(value);
  }

  static left(value) {
    return new Left(value);
  }
}
```

```
class Right extends Either {
  constructor(value) {
    super();
    this.value = value;
  }

  map(fn) {
    return Either.right(fn(this.value));
  }
}

class Left extends Either {
  constructor(value) {
    super();
    this.value = value;
  }

  map(fn) {
    return this;  // Skip further operations
  }
}

// Usage: Validating an email
```

```
const validateEmail = email => email.includes('@') ?
Either.right(email) : Either.left('Invalid email');

const result = validateEmail('example@domain.com')
  .map(email => email.toUpperCase());

console.log(result instanceof Right ? result.value :
result.value);                  //              Output:
'EXAMPLE@DOMAIN.COM'
```

If validation fails, Left is returned and further operations are skipped, creating a safe and readable flow without exceptions.

2. Maybe Type

The Maybe type (often used interchangeably with Option) is used to represent an optional value. It can hold a value or signify its absence without causing errors. The two variations of Maybe are Some (when a value exists) and None (when it doesn't). This approach prevents errors like null pointer exceptions by making absence an explicit state.

Example: Safely accessing nested properties

```javascript
Copy code
class Maybe {
  static some(value) {
    return new Some(value);
  }

  static none() {
    return new None();
  }
}

class Some extends Maybe {
  constructor(value) {
    super();
    this.value = value;
  }

  map(fn) {
    return Maybe.some(fn(this.value));
  }
}

class None extends Maybe {
  map(fn) {
```

```
    return this;  // Skip further operations
  }
}
```

```
// Usage
const getUserCity = user =>
  Maybe.some(user)
    .map(user => user.address)
    .map(address => address.city);
```

```
const user = { name: 'Alice', address: { city:
'Wonderland' } };
const city = getUserCity(user);
console.log(city instanceof Some ? city.value : 'City not
found');  // Output: 'Wonderland'
```

```
const missingUser = null;
const noCity = getUserCity(missingUser);
console.log(noCity instanceof None ? 'City not found' :
noCity.value);  // Output: 'City not found'
```

With Maybe, absent values are handled safely without null checks, preventing runtime errors.

3. Option Type

Option is another way to represent values that may or may not exist, similar to Maybe. In languages like Scala and Rust, Option has two forms: Some for values and None for no values. Using Option, you can explicitly handle cases where values might be missing, encouraging safer code practices.

Example in a Functional-Style Setting:

Extracting optional configuration settings

```javascript
Copy code
class Option {
  static some(value) {
    return new Some(value);
  }

  static none() {
    return new None();
  } I'm
}

class Some extends Option {
  constructor(value) {
```

```
    super();
    this.value = value;
  }

  map(fn) {
    return Option.some(fn(this.value));
  }
}

class None extends Option {
  map(fn) {
    return this;
  }
}

// Example: Fetching configuration data
const getSetting = (config, key) =>
      config[key]   ?   Option.some(config[key])   :
Option.none();

const config = { theme: 'dark' };
const theme = getSetting(config, 'theme')
  .map(value => value.toUpperCase());
```

```
console.log(theme instanceof Some ? theme.value :
'Default theme'); // Output: 'DARK'

const missingSetting = getSetting(config, 'fontSize');
console.log(missingSetting instanceof None ? 'Default
font size' : missingSetting.value); // Output: 'Default
font size'
```

In this example, Option helps us handle configuration settings without risking undefined errors. We use Some or None to express whether a setting is available, eliminating null checks.

Conclusion

Using Either, Maybe, and Option types in functional programming simplifies error handling, missing values, and data validation by making these states explicit. This approach encourages more predictable and safer code by avoiding exceptions and null checks. When chaining operations, these types help bypass unnecessary calculations in error cases, ensuring only valid data proceeds through the pipeline. By adopting these functional types, developers can create resilient and clean code that avoids many common runtime issues.

Handling Errors Functionally in JavaScript

Handling errors functionally in JavaScript involves a structured approach that avoids throwing exceptions, opting instead to manage errors as part of the function's return type. This approach is central to functional programming as it makes error handling predictable, reducing unexpected interruptions and making the code flow smoother. In functional programming, common techniques for handling errors include using monads, chaining functions, and leveraging functional libraries.

1. Using Monads (Maybe and Either)

Monads like Maybe and Either help handle errors by encapsulating results and errors as distinct values, allowing functions to either succeed with a valid result or fail without breaking the code flow. The Maybe monad is useful when a value might be absent, while Either allows differentiation between a successful (Right) and unsuccessful (Left) result.

Example with Either:

javascript
Copy code

```
const divide = (a, b) => (b === 0 ? Either.left("Cannot divide by zero") : Either.right(a / b));

const result = divide(10, 0).map(x => x * 2);

console.log(result);  // Output: Left("Cannot divide by zero")
```

Using Either makes it clear if an operation has failed, and the error can be processed or displayed as needed.

2. Chaining with map and flatMap

Chaining functions with map and flatMap allows the propagation of errors through multiple steps without breaking the code. If an error is encountered in any step, it will carry through, preventing further operations without explicit handling.

```javascript
Copy code
const validate = input => (input ? Either.right(input) : Either.left("Invalid input"));
const process = input => Either.right(input.toUpperCase());

const result = validate("hello")
  .flatMap(process)
  .map(console.log); // Outputs: "HELLO"
```

In this example, if validate returns an error, it will propagate through the chain, ensuring the function doesn't proceed with invalid data.

3. tryCatch Utility for Safe Execution
Wrapping error-prone code in a tryCatch function returns a monadic structure instead of throwing an error, keeping the code functional.

```javascript
Copy code
const tryCatch = fn => {
  try {
    return Either.right(fn());
  } catch (error) {
    return Either.left(error.message);
  }
};

const safeParse = input => tryCatch(() => JSON.parse(input));

console.log(safeParse('{ "key": "value" }'));  // Right({ key: "value" })
console.log(safeParse("invalid   json"));                // Left("Unexpected token i in JSON")
```

This approach eliminates the need for try...catch blocks, letting you handle parsing or other error-prone operations in a declarative style.

4. Using Functional Libraries

Libraries like Ramda, Folktale, and Sanctuary offer utilities for functional error handling, providing tools to work with Maybe, Either, and other structures.

Example with Ramda and Maybe:

```javascript
Copy code
const R = require("ramda");

const safeHead = R.head([]);
console.log(R.isNil(safeHead) ? "No elements" : safeHead); // Output: "No elements"
```

Libraries like these simplify error handling in a functional context, reducing the boilerplate code for safe data access and validation.

Conclusion

Functional error handling in JavaScript ensures a predictable, clean approach to managing exceptions. Using monads, chaining methods, and tryCatch utilities allows JavaScript code to handle errors without disrupting function flow, making the code more maintainable and understandable. Through these techniques, errors are captured, processed, and returned systematically, leading to more robust applications that align with functional programming principles.

Chapter 11
Functional Design Patterns

Functional design patterns are strategies and practices that leverage the core principles of functional programming—such as immutability, pure functions, and higher-order functions—to create clean, maintainable, and reusable code. In JavaScript, these patterns provide a structured approach to designing applications in a more declarative style.

1. Function Composition

Function composition combines smaller functions to build more complex behavior. Instead of creating large, monolithic functions, composition chains together simple functions that handle specific tasks, making the code modular and reusable.

javascript
Copy code
```
const add = x => x + 1;
```

```javascript
const double = x => x * 2;
const addThenDouble = x => double(add(x));

console.log(addThenDouble(3)); // Output: 8
```

2. Currying

Currying transforms functions to take one argument at a time, returning a new function each time until all arguments are received. This pattern allows partial application and can make functions more reusable.

javascript
Copy code
```javascript
const multiply = a => b => a * b;
const double = multiply(2);

console.log(double(3)); // Output: 6
```

3. Higher-order Functions

Higher-order functions take other functions as arguments or return functions, making them ideal for abstraction and code reuse. Examples include map, filter, and reduce, which are commonly used for data transformation.

javascript
Copy code
```
const applyTwice = (fn, value) => fn(fn(value));
console.log(applyTwice(add, 2)); // Output: 4
```

4. Immutability

In functional design, data is immutable, meaning it cannot be modified after creation. Instead, new versions of data are created for changes. This helps avoid side effects and makes functions more predictable.

javascript
Copy code
```
const numbers = [1, 2, 3];
const updatedNumbers = [...numbers, 4];
console.log(updatedNumbers); // Output: [1, 2, 3, 4]
```

5. Monad Pattern

Monads, such as Maybe and Either, handle data with optional or error states, wrapping values in a way that allows chaining operations without breaking the flow. Monads are powerful for handling errors and null values in a functional style.

These functional design patterns help JavaScript developers write modular, scalable, and error-resilient code, following functional programming principles.

Strategy Pattern

The Strategy Pattern is a behavioral design pattern that enables selecting an algorithm's behavior at runtime. Rather than implementing multiple variations of behavior directly in a class or function, the Strategy Pattern encapsulates these behaviors in separate, interchangeable functions or objects.

This pattern is beneficial in functional programming and JavaScript, where functions can be passed as parameters, making it easy to dynamically choose or change behaviors.

Key Concepts of the Strategy Pattern

Encapsulation of Strategies: Each strategy (or algorithm) is encapsulated within a function or class. This makes each behavior modular and reusable.

Interchangeability: Strategies can be swapped in and out at runtime, allowing for flexibility in how an operation is performed without altering the core structure of the code.

Avoids Conditionals: Instead of using conditional statements (like if or switch), the Strategy Pattern dynamically applies the correct algorithm based on a chosen strategy.

Strategy Pattern in JavaScript

In JavaScript, functions are first-class citizens, so the Strategy Pattern is straightforward to implement by passing different functions as strategies.

Example: Payment Processing

Let's say we need a payment system that can handle different types of payments, such as credit card, PayPal, and cryptocurrency. Each payment type is handled by a separate strategy function:

```javascript
Copy code
// Strategy functions for different payment methods
const creditCardPayment = amount => console.log(`Paid $${amount} with Credit Card`);
const payPalPayment = amount => console.log(`Paid $${amount} with PayPal`);
const cryptoPayment = amount => console.log(`Paid $${amount} with Cryptocurrency`);

// Context function to apply the selected payment strategy
const processPayment = (amount, strategy) => strategy(amount);

// Using the Strategy Pattern
processPayment(100, creditCardPayment); // Output: "Paid $100 with Credit Card"
```

```
processPayment(50, payPalPayment);      // Output:
"Paid $50 with PayPal"
processPayment(200, cryptoPayment);     // Output:
"Paid $200 with Cryptocurrency"
```

In this example, each payment type is a different strategy function. The processPayment function dynamically selects which payment method to use by receiving a strategy as a parameter. This keeps the code flexible and avoids conditionals.

Benefits of the Strategy Pattern

Improves Flexibility: New strategies can be added without modifying existing code.

Promotes Code Reusability: Each strategy is a reusable, independent function.

Enhances Maintainability: Reduces clutter and conditionals, making the codebase easier to maintain.

Use Cases

Payment Processing: As shown above, handling different payment types.

Sorting Algorithms: Applying different sorting methods based on data types.

Logging and Notifications: Switching between logging strategies (e.g., to a file, console, or cloud service).

The Strategy Pattern is highly effective in functional programming, where passing functions dynamically is common. It enables cleaner, modular, and easily extensible code in JavaScript applications.

Command Pattern

The Command Pattern is a behavioral design pattern that encapsulates a request or operation as an object, thereby allowing you to parameterize methods with different requests, queue operations, and even support undoable actions. This pattern is particularly useful when you want to decouple the sender (the object that makes a request) from the receiver (the object that performs the action) and give more control over how and when commands are executed.

In JavaScript, the Command Pattern is implemented by creating command objects that contain all the information needed to perform an action. Each command object typically has methods like execute (to perform the action) and undo (to reverse the action).

Key Components of the Command Pattern

Command: The interface or base class defining the execute and undo methods.
Concrete Command: Implements the Command interface, defines the action, and stores any necessary information to perform it.
Invoker: The object that calls the execute method of a command.
Receiver: The object that actually performs the action, often accessed through the command.

Command Pattern in JavaScript

Here's an example where we use the Command Pattern to control operations in a simple text editor, allowing us to perform and undo text commands.

Example: Text Editor with Undoable Commands

```javascript
Copy code
// Receiver class
class TextEditor {
  constructor() {
    this.content = "";
  }
  addText(text) {
    this.content += text;
  }
  removeText(text) {
    this.content = this.content.replace(text, "");
  }
  getContent() {
    return this.content;
  }
}

// Command interface
class Command {
  execute() {}
  undo() {}
}
```

```javascript
// Concrete Command for adding text
class AddTextCommand extends Command {
  constructor(editor, text) {
    super();
    this.editor = editor;
    this.text = text;
  }
  execute() {
    this.editor.addText(this.text);
  }
  undo() {
    this.editor.removeText(this.text);
  }
}

// Invoker class
class CommandManager {
  constructor() {
    this.history = [];
  }
  executeCommand(command) {
    command.execute();
    this.history.push(command);
  }
```

```javascript
  undo() {
    const command = this.history.pop();
    if (command) {
      command.undo();
    }
  }
}

// Usage
const editor = new TextEditor();
const commandManager = new CommandManager();

const addHello = new AddTextCommand(editor,
"Hello, ");
const addWorld = new AddTextCommand(editor,
"world!");

commandManager.executeCommand(addHello);
commandManager.executeCommand(addWorld);

console.log(editor.getContent()); // Output: "Hello,
world!"

commandManager.undo();
console.log(editor.getContent()); // Output: "Hello, "
```

In this example:

Receiver: TextEditor class, which performs actions like adding or removing text.

Concrete Command: AddTextCommand class, which encapsulates the action to add or remove text.

Invoker: CommandManager class, which executes commands and keeps track of the history for undo functionality.

The Command Pattern allows us to issue commands to the text editor, queue them, and even undo them. This pattern is valuable in applications that require complex actions to be reversible or where commands can be executed in different orders.

Benefits of the Command Pattern

Encapsulates Actions as Objects: Making it easy to extend or modify command behaviors.

Enables Undo/Redo Functionality: By keeping a history of commands.

Decouples Command Sender and Receiver: Increasing modularity and flexibility in code.

Use Cases

Undoable Operations: Text editors, image editors, or any software requiring reversible actions.

Macro Recording: In games or applications where users can record and replay actions.

Transaction Systems: Banking or e-commerce systems where requests can be queued and executed in order.

The Command Pattern in JavaScript offers a robust structure for handling operations in a decoupled and organized manner, making it ideal for any application requiring complex or reversible actions.

Using Functional Patterns in JavaScript Applications

Functional patterns in JavaScript offer a modern, clean, and scalable approach to application development. These patterns focus on immutability, pure functions, and composable structures, allowing developers to create applications that are easier to maintain, debug, and reason about. By adopting functional programming principles, JavaScript developers can enhance code modularity, testability, and reuse.

Key Functional Patterns in JavaScript

Pure Functions

Pure functions are functions that, given the same inputs, always produce the same output and have no side effects (they don't alter any external state). Pure functions make testing easier and help reduce bugs, as they don't depend on or alter any outside data.

javascript
Copy code
```
const add = (a, b) => a + b; // Pure function
```

Immutability

Functional applications strive to avoid mutating data. Instead of changing objects or arrays, new versions are created with the desired updates. This reduces unexpected side effects and makes code behavior more predictable.

javascript
Copy code

```javascript
const numbers = [1, 2, 3];
const updatedNumbers = [...numbers, 4]; // Creates a new array with added element
```

Higher-order Functions

Higher-order functions (HOFs) take other functions as arguments or return functions as results. Common HOFs in JavaScript include map, filter, and reduce, which are used extensively for transforming and processing arrays.

javascript
Copy code

```javascript
const double = x => x * 2;
const numbers = [1, 2, 3];
const doubled = numbers.map(double); // [2, 4, 6]
```

Function Composition

Function composition is a pattern where multiple functions are combined to create a new function that performs a sequence of operations. This pattern promotes modularity and reuse by breaking down complex operations into smaller, reusable functions.

javascript
Copy code
```javascript
const add = x => x + 1;
const double = x => x * 2;
const addThenDouble = x => double(add(x));
```

Currying

Currying transforms a function with multiple arguments into a series of functions that each take a single argument. This enables partial application, allowing you to fix some arguments and create specialized functions from general-purpose ones.

javascript
Copy code

```javascript
const multiply = a => b => a * b;
const double = multiply(2);
console.log(double(5)); // Output: 10
```

Monad and Functor Patterns

Monads and functors handle data with optional or error states, allowing safe and flexible chaining of operations without null or undefined errors. A common monad in JavaScript is Promise, which encapsulates an asynchronous computation.

javascript
Copy code
```javascript
const fetchData = url => fetch(url).then(response => response.json());
```

Applying Functional Patterns in Real-World Applications
Functional patterns can greatly benefit applications by making complex code easier to manage and refactor. Here are a few ways functional patterns can be applied in JavaScript:

Data Transformation Pipelines: Data processing tasks like transforming API responses or filtering data can be simplified using map, filter, reduce, and function composition.

javascript
Copy code
```
const data = [1, 2, 3, 4];
const result = data
  .filter(x => x > 2)
  .map(x => x * 2);
// Output: [6, 8]
```

Event Handling in User Interfaces: Higher-order functions and currying can manage event handlers, separating the logic from the implementation.

javascript
Copy code
```
const handleClick = id => () => console.log(`Clicked ${id}`);
document.getElementById('button1').addEventListener('click', handleClick(1));
```

Error Handling with Either/Maybe: Using functional patterns to encapsulate potential errors, developers can avoid throwing exceptions and instead return data in a consistent format, using monads to handle nullable or error-prone operations.

Functional patterns in JavaScript allow developers to build applications that are scalable, reliable, and resilient to errors. By leveraging these principles, JavaScript code becomes more predictable and modular, supporting long-term maintainability and performance.

Chapter 12
Asynchronous Functional Programming

Asynchronous functional programming combines functional principles with asynchronous operations, allowing JavaScript applications to handle complex workflows and data flows in a clean, non-blocking way. This approach uses concepts like promises, async/await, and higher-order functions to manage asynchronous actions without side effects or mutations, aligning with the functional programming goal of immutability.

Key Concepts in Asynchronous Functional Programming

Promises: Promises provide a way to handle asynchronous operations as values that can be chained and composed. Functions like .then(), .catch(), and .finally() enable handling asynchronous events in a functional way.

javascript

```
const fetchData = url => fetch(url).then(response =>
response.json());
fetchData('https://api.example.com/data').then(data
=> console.log(data));
```

Async/Await: Async functions provide a cleaner syntax for working with promises, making asynchronous code easier to read and write while retaining the functional approach.

javascript

```
const fetchData = async url => {
  const response = await fetch(url);
  return response.json();
};
```

Higher-Order Asynchronous Functions: Functions like Promise.all, Promise.race, and user-defined higher-order functions enable composing multiple async operations. This makes it easier to handle complex workflows, like waiting for multiple asynchronous tasks to complete.

javascript

```
const       fetchData    =    async    url    =>    await
fetch(url).then(res => res.json());
const    fetchMultipleData    =    async    urls    =>
Promise.all(urls.map(fetchData));
```

Immutability and Statelessness:

Asynchronous functional programming emphasizes avoiding shared state and mutable data, making it easier to reason about code that handles multiple concurrent operations without race conditions or side effects.

Benefits of Asynchronous Functional Programming

Readability: Async/await and promise chaining lead to cleaner, more readable code.

Modularity: Asynchronous functions can be easily composed and reused, which is especially useful in large applications.

Error Handling: Functional patterns like .catch() in promises enable structured, modular error handling, which helps manage errors in complex async flows.

Asynchronous functional programming allows JavaScript applications to handle complex asynchronous workflows while preserving the benefits of functional programming—cleaner code, modularity, and more predictable behavior.

Promises and Functional Programming

Promises in JavaScript provide a powerful way to handle asynchronous operations in a functional style, allowing developers to write clean, non-blocking code. Promises represent a value that may not be available yet (e.g., data from an API call) and offer a structured way to manage async operations by chaining functions.

How Promises Align with Functional Programming

In functional programming, functions are typically pure and avoid side effects, focusing on transformations from input to output. Promises align well with this paradigm by enabling functional-style operations such as chaining and composing functions for async tasks, which helps maintain clean, predictable code flow.

Chaining with .then(): Promises support chaining, where each .then() handler receives the result of the previous step, allowing complex workflows to be built with simple, reusable functions. This chaining makes code more modular and avoids deeply nested callbacks, known as "callback hell."

```javascript
Copy code
const fetchData = url =>
  fetch(url)
    .then(response => response.json())
    .then(data => console.log(data))
    .catch(error => console.error("Error:", error));
```

Higher-Order Promises: In functional programming, higher-order functions (functions that take other functions as arguments or return them) are common. Similarly, higher-order promise functions like Promise.all or Promise.race allow combining multiple promises, enabling parallel and race conditions to be managed declaratively.

```javascript
Copy code
```

```
const        fetchAllData        =        urls        =>
Promise.all(urls.map(fetchData));
```

Avoiding Side Effects: Promises work well with pure functions, which have no side effects and produce the same output given the same input. By combining promises with pure functions, developers can manage async data transformations without changing external state, which leads to more predictable, testable code.

Error Handling with .catch(): Functional programming promotes modular and consistent error handling. With promises, .catch() enables centralized handling of async errors, which reduces error-handling logic scattered throughout the codebase.

```javascript
Copy code
fetchData('https://api.example.com/data')
  .then(processData) // processData is a pure function
  .catch(handleError); // handleError is a reusable error handler
```

Functional Benefits of Using Promises

Modularity: With promises, asynchronous operations can be modularized into small, composable functions, making it easier to reuse and test each part.

Readability: Promises improve readability by removing the need for nested callbacks and providing a linear flow of operations.

Predictability: By maintaining functional principles like purity and immutability, promises help make async code easier to understand and debug.

Example: Fetching and Transforming Data

Consider an example where a promise is used to fetch data and apply transformations using functional principles.

```javascript
Copy code
const fetchData = url =>
  fetch(url)
    .then(response => response.json())
    .then(data => data.map(transformData))
    .catch(error => console.error("Error:", error));
```

Here, transformData is a pure function that's applied to each element in data, showing how promises allow for modular, functional handling of async operations.

Conclusion

Promises align well with functional programming by enabling modular, predictable, and readable async code. With promise-based chaining, higher-order functions, and centralized error handling, JavaScript promises make it easier to apply functional principles to async workflows. This approach enhances code quality, making applications more scalable and maintainable.

Async/Await in Functional Code

The async/await syntax in JavaScript provides a more readable and linear way to handle asynchronous operations, making it a natural fit for functional programming. By wrapping asynchronous tasks in functions that return promises, async/await helps achieve clean, predictable, and modular code. It also enables developers to apply functional programming principles to async code, enhancing readability and reusability while reducing complexity.

How Async/Await Aligns with Functional Programming

Improved Readability and Flow: Unlike traditional promise chaining, which can become complex when chaining many .then() statements, async/await provides a synchronous-looking syntax that is easier to read and understand. This readability promotes modular, functional code, where each async operation is clearly separated and flows in a natural sequence.

```javascript
Copy code
const fetchData = async (url) => {
  const response = await fetch(url);
  const data = await response.json();
  return data;
};
```

Composability: Functional programming emphasizes composing small, pure functions into larger functions. With async/await, asynchronous functions can be composed more easily. Each async function can return a promise, allowing other functions to await its result and combine multiple async tasks in a functional manner.

javascript
Copy code
```
const getData = async (url1, url2) => {
    const [data1, data2] = await Promise.all([fetchData(url1), fetchData(url2)]);
    return processData(data1, data2); // processData is a pure function
};
```

Error Handling with Try/Catch: Error handling in async/await is more straightforward and fits well with functional principles. Using try/catch blocks around await calls allows for modular error handling, where each async function can manage its errors independently or pass them up the chain. This centralized error handling reduces side effects and improves code readability.

javascript
Copy code
```
const fetchData = async (url) => {
  try {
    const response = await fetch(url);
```

```
    if (!response.ok) throw new Error('Network
response was not ok');
    return await response.json();
  } catch (error) {
    console.error('Fetch error:', error);
  }
};
```

Avoiding Side Effects: Functional

programming aims to minimize side effects. With
async/await, async functions can return values instead of
altering external state. By using immutability and avoiding
shared state, async/await aligns with functional principles by
keeping async functions isolated and predictable.

Higher-Order Asynchronous Functions:

With async/await, you can create higher-order functions
that return or modify async functions. For example, you
could create a retryAsync function that takes an async
function and retries it on failure, making it easier to
compose async tasks functionally.

javascript

Copy code

```javascript
const retryAsync = (asyncFunc, retries = 3) => async (...args) => {
  for (let i = 0; i < retries; i++) {
    try {
      return await asyncFunc(...args);
    } catch (error) {
      if (i === retries - 1) throw error;
    }
  }
};
```

Benefits of Using Async/Await in Functional Code

Improved Modularity: Each async function can be written as a small, reusable unit, making code more modular.

Better Debugging and Error Handling: Using try/catch with async/await simplifies error handling and allows for cleaner debugging.

Enhanced Composition: Async functions can be easily composed, combined, and passed as arguments to other functions, enabling more functional, declarative code.

Example: Processing and Composing Async Functions
Consider a functional async workflow where data is fetched
from an API and processed in a pipeline:

```javascript
Copy code
const fetchData = async (url) => {
  const response = await fetch(url);
  return response.json();
};

const processData = async (url) => {
  const data = await fetchData(url);
  return data.map(transformData); // transformData is
a pure function
};
```

With async/await, each function remains modular,
predictable, and easy to compose, fitting perfectly within a
functional style of programming.

Conclusion

The async/await syntax is a powerful tool for writing functional asynchronous code in JavaScript. By improving readability, modularity, and error handling, async/await supports functional programming principles, making asynchronous code easier to maintain, test, and scale.

Using Functional Patterns for Asynchronous Workflows

In JavaScript, applying functional patterns to asynchronous workflows brings structure, modularity, and readability to code that deals with non-blocking tasks. By treating asynchronous operations with a functional approach, developers can create predictable and maintainable workflows that are easier to compose, test, and debug.

Key Functional Patterns in Asynchronous Workflows

Promise Chaining and Composition: Promise chaining allows asynchronous functions to be composed in a linear, functional style. Each function in the chain takes the result of the previous one, creating a pipeline where data flows through transformations. This pattern supports modularity by isolating each step, making it easier to test and reuse.

javascript
Copy code

```javascript
fetchData(url)
  .then(parseData)     // parseData is a pure function
    .then(validateData)      // validateData is a pure function
      .catch(handleError);   // handleError is a reusable error handler
```

Higher-Order Asynchronous Functions: Higher-order functions are a core concept in functional programming and can be applied to async workflows. By creating functions that return other async functions, we enable flexibility and customization. A common use is a retryAsync function that takes an async function and retries it on failure, which is useful for handling network calls.

javascript

Copy code

```
const retryAsync = (asyncFunc, retries = 3) => async
(...args) => {
  for (let i = 0; i < retries; i++) {
    try {
      return await asyncFunc(...args);
    } catch (error) {
      if (i === retries - 1) throw error;
    }
  }
};
```

Parallelism with Promise.all and Promise.race: Functional programming often involves working with collections of data, and async workflows are no different. With Promise.all, multiple async operations can be executed in parallel, while Promise.race returns the result of the fastest promise. Both allow developers to handle asynchronous operations declaratively, which is helpful for functional pipelines that require concurrent data fetching.

javascript
Copy code

```
const fetchMultipleData = async (urls) => {
```

```javascript
const data = await Promise.all(urls.map(fetchData));
// fetchData is a reusable async function
  return data.map(transformData); // transformData is
a pure function
};
```

Using async/await in Function Composition: The async/await syntax makes composing async functions more natural and readable. By composing async functions sequentially, workflows can be created that resemble synchronous code but remain non-blocking. This linear style improves readability and lets functions like map or reduce process data in an async manner.

```javascript
javascript
Copy code
const processData = async (url) => {
  const rawData = await fetchData(url);
    const parsedData = await parseData(rawData); //
parseData is a pure async function
    return transformData(parsedData);              //
transformData is a pure function
};
```

Monads for Error Handling (e.g., Either, Maybe): Functional programming often uses monads, such as Either or Maybe, to manage errors in a pipeline without disrupting flow. While JavaScript doesn't have built-in monads, libraries like folktale and ramda implement them, allowing developers to wrap async functions in Either or Maybe monads. This approach helps keep error handling consistent and avoids side effects.

Functional Error Handling with try/catch Blocks: Using try/catch with async/await improves error handling by keeping it centralized, which is a key aspect of functional programming. Instead of scattering error-handling logic across multiple locations, developers can wrap workflows in try/catch, handling all errors in one place without side effects.

```javascript
Copy code
const fetchDataWithHandling = async (url) => {
  try {
    const data = await fetchData(url);
    return transformData(data);
  } catch (error) {
```

```
        handleError(error); // handleError is a pure error
handler
  }
};
```

Benefits of Functional Patterns in Async Workflows

Modularity: Functional patterns break down async
workflows into smaller, reusable components, making them
easier to test and debug.

Predictability: Avoiding side effects and using pure
functions keeps each async operation predictable and
minimizes unexpected behaviors.

Scalability: With higher-order async functions, workflows
can be scaled easily to handle various async tasks without
duplication.

Improved Error Handling: Using monads or centralized
try/catch blocks enables more graceful error handling in
async code, helping to create resilient applications.

Example: Composing Async Workflows with Functional
Patterns

Consider an example of using Promise.all for a simple functional async workflow:

javascript
Copy code

```javascript
const fetchAndProcessData = async (urls) => {
  const results = await Promise.all(urls.map(async (url) => {
    try {
      const data = await fetchData(url);
      return processData(data);
    } catch (error) {
      return handleError(error); // handleError returns a default value or logs
    }
  }));
  return results;
};
```

In this example:

Promise.all enables parallel fetching of data from multiple URLs.
Each URL fetch is processed using a reusable processData function.

Errors are handled functionally, ensuring consistent error handling without disrupting the workflow.

Conclusion

Applying functional patterns to asynchronous workflows in JavaScript offers structure, readability, and maintainability. By composing small, reusable async functions, handling errors centrally, and leveraging higher-order and parallel functions, developers can build scalable and predictable async applications. These functional principles enable clean, modular code that's better suited for complex, real-world applications.

PART V: BUILDING APPLICATIONS WITH FUNCTIONAL PARADIGM

Chapter 13
Building Reusable Components

Creating reusable components in JavaScript involves designing small, single-purpose functions or modules that can easily adapt to various contexts. By focusing on modularity and avoiding dependencies on specific data or states, reusable components allow for flexibility and maintainability.

Reusable components often rely on principles like immutability, pure functions, and higher-order functions. For example, a reusable fetchData function could handle API calls without being tied to a specific URL or data transformation, while a formatDate utility could work consistently across different parts of an application. These components improve code consistency, make testing simpler, and reduce the need for duplicated logic.

Structuring Code for Reusability

Structuring code for reusability is about organizing your application in a way that promotes modularity, flexibility, and scalability. This ensures that components or functions can be reused across different parts of the application without unnecessary duplication. Effective code reuse improves maintainability, reduces errors, and allows developers to make changes to one part of the code without affecting other areas.

Here are key practices for structuring code for reusability:

Modularization: Break the application into smaller, independent modules or components that each focus on a single task. These modules should be self-contained, meaning they only interact with other modules through clearly defined interfaces. For example, in JavaScript, creating utility functions (e.g., formatDate, fetchData) that are decoupled from specific application logic makes them reusable in different parts of the app.

Pure Functions: Design functions that don't rely on external state or cause side effects. Pure functions return the same output for the same input, making them predictable and easy to reuse in different scenarios without unintended consequences. For instance, a function that transforms a user object into a greeting message can be reused wherever needed without any side effects.

Higher-order Functions: These functions take other functions as arguments or return functions. Higher-order functions enable the creation of reusable patterns, such as mapping, filtering, or reducing data. For example, a higher-order function like map can be used to apply any transformation to an array, making it highly reusable.

Separation of Concerns: Keep the logic for different concerns (e.g., UI, data manipulation, business logic) separate. This modular structure allows individual components to be reused in different contexts without interference from other parts of the application. For example, separating data-fetching logic from UI rendering allows both to be reused independently.

Avoiding Hard-Coding: Instead of hard-coding values or behaviors directly in functions or components, pass parameters or use configuration options to make components flexible. For instance, instead of writing a component that only works with a specific dataset, pass the dataset as an argument so the component can work with any data.

Abstraction and Interfaces: Define clear interfaces for your modules or components. This abstraction hides the implementation details while exposing only necessary functions, making it easier to reuse the component without understanding its internal workings.

Testing and Documentation:

Well-documented and thoroughly tested reusable components are easier to maintain and share. Clear documentation explains how to use a component, and tests ensure it works correctly across different scenarios, making the component reliable and reusable.

By following these practices, developers can build applications that are flexible, easier to maintain, and more adaptable to future changes, all while minimizing duplication and enhancing productivity.

Composing Components Functionally

Composing components functionally involves combining small, pure, and independent functions or components to build more complex behavior. The goal is to create flexible, reusable components that can be composed together in various configurations to produce desired results. This functional approach encourages immutability, simplicity, and clarity in code design.

Here are key principles for composing components functionally:

Modularity: Create components that handle a single responsibility or task. Each function or component should be small and focused, making it easier to reuse and combine with others. For example, a component that formats dates can be composed with other components that fetch or display data, creating complex functionalities from simpler pieces.

Function Composition: This involves chaining or combining pure functions together. By passing the output of one function as the input to another, developers can build complex logic from simple, reusable components. In JavaScript, this can be done using higher-order functions like compose or pipe. For instance, a series of functions that filter, transform, and sort data can be composed into a single function that processes data step-by-step.

Immutability: When composing components, ensure that the state is not mutated. This means each function should return a new value rather than modifying the original data. For example, a transformation function that creates a new list based on an existing one rather than altering the original list promotes safer and more predictable compositions.

Higher-order Components (HOCs): In frameworks like React, higher-order components can be used to compose functionality in a reusable manner. HOCs are functions that take a component and return a new component, adding additional behavior. This functional composition allows for combining various concerns (e.g., authentication, logging) into existing components without modifying their core logic.

Declarative Programming: Rather than focusing on how a task is performed, functional composition allows you to express what needs to be done, letting the composition of functions handle the details. This leads to more readable and maintainable code.

Separation of Concerns: When composing components functionally, each component should be responsible for a specific concern (e.g., data fetching, UI rendering, user interactions). This separation makes it easier to combine components and swap out parts without breaking the overall functionality.

Reusability and Scalability: Functional composition naturally promotes reusability. By designing components that focus on specific tasks, you can easily compose them in various ways to meet new requirements. For example, a filtering function can be combined with different sorting and mapping functions, making it reusable in various parts of the application.

Composable Error Handling: In functional composition, handling errors can be done by returning Maybe, Either, or other functional data structures that represent possible failures. This keeps the flow of the program consistent and easy to reason about, as errors are handled within the composition rather than interrupting it.

By composing components functionally, you can build complex systems from smaller, simpler building blocks. This approach promotes clean, maintainable, and scalable code, allowing you to focus on solving problems without getting bogged down in the details of individual components.

Testing and Debugging Functional Code

Testing and debugging functional code involves ensuring that individual functions and components behave as expected, remain pure, and can be composed reliably. Since functional programming emphasizes immutability, purity, and declarative logic, it offers certain advantages for testing, such as making functions easier to isolate and reason about. However, it also introduces unique challenges that require tailored approaches to testing and debugging.

Key Strategies for Testing Functional Code:

Unit Testing Pure Functions: In functional programming, pure functions are predictable because they always produce the same output for the same input and don't cause side effects. This predictability makes unit testing easier, as you can simply test the function's output for different inputs without worrying about external factors. Frameworks like Mocha, Jest, or Jasmine are commonly used for unit testing in JavaScript.

Example: If you have a pure function like add(a, b), you can write simple tests to ensure it returns the correct sum for various input values.

Mocking and Stubbing: When testing higher-order functions or components that depend on external resources (e.g., APIs, databases), it's important to mock or stub out those dependencies. In functional programming, mocking can be done in a way that does not interfere with the purity of functions. This allows you to test logic without invoking actual external services, making tests faster and more predictable.

Example: Mocking a network request in a higher-order function to test its behavior without actually making an API call.

Property-based Testing: Functional code often focuses on defining properties or relationships (e.g., "applying a filter and then a map function should give the same result as mapping and then filtering"). Property-based testing tools, like FastCheck for JavaScript, automatically generate a variety of inputs to test that these properties hold true for your functions. This allows you to test a wide range of cases, including edge cases, which can be challenging to anticipate.

Testing Composability: When composing functions together, you should test that the composed functions interact correctly. This can be done by writing tests for smaller functions and then composing them in test cases. For example, testing a map function composed with filter ensures that the order of transformations does not introduce unexpected behavior.

Edge Case Handling: Testing functional code also requires attention to edge cases, such as empty lists, null values, and invalid inputs. Since functional programming encourages handling such cases explicitly (often using Maybe, Either, or

Option types), you can write tests to ensure that edge cases are handled gracefully without causing runtime errors.

Example: Testing a function that safely handles null or undefined inputs using Option types or default values.
Debugging Functional Code: Debugging functional code can be trickier than debugging imperative code due to its abstract nature. However, the use of pure functions and immutability makes it easier to reason about code. To debug functional code:

Use Logs and Tracing: Since functional code tends to avoid side effects, inserting logs or using debugging tools like the browser's built-in debugger or tools like VSCode breakpoints can help inspect function inputs and outputs at different stages of the program.

Function Breakdown: Break down complex composed functions into smaller, isolated units. Debugging smaller pieces of logic is simpler than debugging large, interconnected code blocks.

Immutability Check: Ensure that data structures aren't being mutated unexpectedly. Tools like Immutable.js or

Immer help maintain immutability and can provide useful debugging insights when things go wrong.

Use of Types for Debugging: Leveraging strong typing (e.g., using TypeScript or Flow in JavaScript) can catch errors at compile time, preventing many runtime issues. Type systems help detect issues early, such as passing incorrect types to functions or using undefined variables.

Example: Type annotations in TypeScript can help ensure that the correct types are passed to functions, preventing type-related bugs in functional code.

Functional Patterns for Error Handling: In functional programming, errors are typically handled through constructs like Maybe, Either, or Result types. These allow you to explicitly handle error cases without throwing exceptions or causing program crashes. During testing, you should ensure these error-handling patterns behave as expected.

Example: Testing a function that returns an Either type to handle errors or success states properly, ensuring both branches of the result (success or failure) are covered.

Conclusion

Testing and debugging functional code involves leveraging the inherent properties of functional programming, such as pure functions, immutability, and higher-order functions, to create predictable and maintainable systems. By using unit tests, property-based testing, mock dependencies, and debugging techniques tailored for functional code, you can ensure that your functions behave correctly and compose well together. Additionally, functional patterns for error handling, such as Maybe and Either, provide an elegant way to manage errors without disrupting the flow of the program.

Chapter 14

State Management in Functional Applications

State management in functional programming emphasizes immutability, pure functions, and declarative updates. Instead of directly modifying state, functional applications create new versions of the state, ensuring predictability and avoiding side effects.

Key principles include:

Immutability: State is never directly mutated; new copies are created with necessary updates.
Pure Functions: Functions that return a new state based on the current state and actions without side effects.
Declarative Updates: State transitions are declared, and the system determines how to update the state.

Action-Based Models: State changes are triggered by actions (e.g., user interactions), handled by pure functions (e.g., reducers).

Techniques include reducer patterns (e.g., Redux), monads (e.g., State Monad), and Functional Reactive Programming (FRP). These approaches help create predictable, testable, and maintainable state management systems, where state is passed through functions, and changes are consistent and traceable.

Functional Approaches to State

In functional programming, state management is handled differently from traditional imperative approaches. The key idea is to treat state as immutable and to use pure functions to manage transitions, which ensures that state changes are predictable, traceable, and free from unintended side effects.

Key Principles of Functional State Management

Immutability: In functional programming, state is not changed directly. Instead, any change results in a new state being returned, leaving the original state intact. This ensures that there is no accidental mutation, and state remains consistent across the application.

Example: If a state is { counter: 0 }, an increment operation returns a new state like { counter: 1 }, instead of modifying the original state.

Pure Functions: State transitions are managed by pure functions, which take the current state and an action (or event) as input and return a new state. These functions do not modify the state or have side effects, making them predictable and easy to test.

Example: A pure reducer function could look like this:

```javascript
Copy code
function counterReducer(state, action) {
  if (action.type === 'INCREMENT') {
    return { counter: state.counter + 1 };
  }
  return state;
```

}

Declarative Approach: Functional programming emphasizes declaring what should be done with the state rather than how to do it. The system takes care of the state updates and ensures they happen in a consistent and predictable manner.

Action-based or Event-driven: In functional applications, state changes are typically driven by actions or events (e.g., user interactions, network responses). The state is updated only in response to these triggers, often through the use of a reducer or a similar pure function.

Techniques for Managing State Functionally

Reducer Pattern: A common technique is the use of reducers, where a pure function computes a new state based on an action. This pattern is widely used in state management libraries like Redux.

Example: A reducer might receive an action like INCREMENT and return a new state based on the previous state:

javascript

Copy code

```
function rootReducer(state = { counter: 0 }, action) {
  switch(action.type) {
    case 'INCREMENT':
     return { counter: state.counter + 1 };
    default:
     return state;
  }
}
```

Monads: Monads, especially the State Monad, encapsulate state and allow for easy chaining of state transformations. The State Monad simplifies the handling of state, avoiding direct mutation while maintaining composability and readability.

Functional Reactive Programming (FRP): FRP is a paradigm that combines functional programming with reactive programming. State is modeled as streams of data that can be observed and transformed. Libraries like RxJS or Most.js allow functional handling of asynchronous events and state changes.

Persistent Data Structures: Functional applications often use persistent (or immutable) data structures, where new versions of the data are created with each change, while the original data remains intact. This allows for safe concurrent access and changes to the state.

Context-based Propagation: In frameworks like React, the Context API is used to propagate state throughout the application. State is passed through the context, and components consume it without needing to explicitly pass it as props, maintaining a clean and functional architecture.

Advantages of Functional State Management

Predictability: Since state transitions are handled by pure functions, the resulting state is always predictable and easier to debug.

Testability: Pure functions can be tested independently, making unit tests simpler and more effective.

Immutability: State cannot be accidentally mutated, leading to fewer bugs related to shared state.

Composition: Functional state management techniques like reducers and monads allow for easy composition of smaller state transition functions to create more complex ones.

Conclusion

Functional approaches to state management leverage immutability, pure functions, and declarative programming to create predictable, reliable, and testable systems. By using techniques like the reducer pattern, monads, and functional reactive programming, developers can effectively manage state without the complications of mutable data, leading to more maintainable applications.

Managing State in Complex Applications

In complex applications, state management becomes increasingly challenging due to the growing number of components, data sources, and user interactions. Effectively managing state is crucial to maintaining performance, ensuring consistency, and providing a seamless user experience. Functional programming provides powerful strategies and patterns for managing state in a declarative, predictable, and immutable way.

Key Considerations for State Management in Complex Applications

Immutability: In complex applications, managing state immutably is crucial to avoiding unintended side effects and ensuring that state changes are predictable. Each update to the state should create a new version of the state rather than modifying the existing one. This reduces complexity and makes it easier to track and debug changes.

State Partitioning: As the size and complexity of the application grow, the application's state often needs to be partitioned into smaller, more manageable pieces. These partitions should ideally reflect the structure and concerns of the application (e.g., UI state, business logic, network state, etc.).

Centralized vs. Distributed State: In large applications, the decision between using centralized or distributed state management is important:

Centralized State: Libraries like Redux or MobX provide centralized stores that hold the entire application state. This makes it easier to track and debug state changes but can become a bottleneck in very large applications.

Distributed State: Some applications prefer to keep state localized within individual components, passing data down the component tree. This approach scales well but can lead to redundancy and complexity in syncing state between components.

Normalization: In applications with nested or deeply structured data, normalization is often used to flatten the state into a more manageable format. By storing related entities in separate collections and referencing them by ID, we avoid the complexity of deeply nested state and make it easier to update and access related data.

Strategies for Managing Complex State

Reducer Pattern: As the application grows, the reducer pattern is a powerful way to manage complex state transitions. The state is modified in a predictable way through pure functions called reducers. Each reducer handles a specific part of the state, allowing for easy composition and decoupling of state concerns.

Example: In a complex app with different concerns (e.g., user data, products, and settings), separate reducers could handle each concern:

javascript

Copy code
```
function userReducer(state = {}, action) {
  switch (action.type) {
    case 'SET_USER':
      return { ...state, user: action.payload };
    default:
      return state;
  }
}

function productsReducer(state = [], action) {
  switch (action.type) {
    case 'SET_PRODUCTS':
      return action.payload;
    default:
      return state;
  }
}
```

State Management Libraries: For complex applications, libraries like Redux, MobX, or Zustand help manage state across many components. These libraries provide centralized state storage, action dispatching, and reactivity, making it easier to coordinate state changes in large applications.

Redux uses actions and reducers to update the state, while providing tools like middleware to handle asynchronous actions.

MobX focuses on reactivity and uses observables, making state changes more declarative and reducing boilerplate.

Zustand is a simpler, minimalistic state management library that leverages hooks for managing state.

State Persistence: In complex applications, it's important to persist state across sessions (e.g., user preferences, form data). This can be achieved using techniques like:

Local Storage or Session Storage to store key-value pairs in the browser.

IndexedDB for larger datasets that need to persist across sessions.

Server-Side State to store state on the server and sync it with the client-side application.

State Synchronization: In modern applications, state may need to be synchronized across multiple components or between the client and server. Techniques such as WebSockets, GraphQL subscriptions, or Polling can be used to ensure the application remains up-to-date with real-time data changes.

Side Effects and Middleware: Managing side effects (e.g., API calls, timers, animations) is crucial in complex applications. Middleware (e.g., Redux-Saga, Redux-Thunk, or RxJS) provides a structured way to handle these side effects while keeping them separate from state logic, ensuring that the application's core state management remains pure.

Error Handling: In large applications, error handling becomes complex. Functional programming techniques such as Either and Maybe types can be used to represent the success or failure of operations and manage errors in a declarative way.

Example: A network request might return an Either type, which can either be a Right with the response data or a Left with an error message.

Managing Asynchronous State

Complex applications often rely on asynchronous operations like fetching data from APIs or processing user interactions. Functional patterns can help manage asynchronous state in a way that integrates seamlessly with the rest of the application:

Promises and Async/Await are used to handle asynchronous operations while ensuring that state transitions are managed in a predictable manner.

Functional Reactive Programming (FRP) allows applications to work with streams of data (like real-time updates) and react to state changes asynchronously, leading to more declarative code.

Performance Optimization

As applications scale, performance optimizations become essential. Techniques such as memoization and lazy loading can be used to avoid unnecessary state recalculations and improve the efficiency of state updates.

Memoization: Caching results of expensive computations based on the current state can improve performance by avoiding repeated calculations.

Lazy Loading: Only loading state or components when they are needed (e.g., in a paginated list or when the user interacts with certain features) helps reduce the initial load time and resource consumption.

Conclusion

Managing state in complex applications requires careful planning and the application of functional principles like immutability, pure functions, and declarative updates. By using patterns like reducers, state management libraries, and handling asynchronous state, developers can create scalable, maintainable applications. Additionally, techniques such as state persistence, synchronization, and optimization ensure that state management remains efficient as the application grows. With these strategies, complex applications can remain predictable, testable, and easy to debug.

Using Libraries like Redux with Functional Patterns

In modern JavaScript applications, state management is a critical concern, especially when the application becomes complex. Libraries like Redux have become widely adopted for managing global state in a predictable and scalable way. When using Redux with functional programming patterns, you can leverage the power of immutability, pure functions, and composability to build maintainable and efficient applications. Here's how Redux can integrate with functional patterns:

Redux Basics

Redux is a state management library that follows the Flux architecture, providing a predictable state container for JavaScript apps. It works around three core concepts:

Actions: Plain JavaScript objects that represent an intention to change the state.

Reducers: Pure functions that specify how the state changes in response to an action.

Store: Holds the application's state and manages its updates via actions and reducers.

Combining Redux with Functional Programming Principles

Functional programming (FP) emphasizes immutability, pure functions, declarative code, and higher-order functions, all of which can enhance how you manage state in Redux.

1. Immutability

In Redux, the state is immutable, meaning the state should never be directly modified. Instead, a new state is returned from the reducer function when an action is dispatched. This aligns with functional programming, where immutability is a core principle.

Example: A reducer in Redux should never mutate the state directly; instead, it should return a new object or array when making updates.

```javascript
Copy code
const initialState = { counter: 0 };

function counterReducer(state = initialState, action) {
```

```
switch (action.type) {
  case 'INCREMENT':
    return { ...state, counter: state.counter + 1 };
  case 'DECREMENT':
    return { ...state, counter: state.counter - 1 };
  default:
    return state;
  }
}
```

This approach ensures that the state changes are predictable and avoids side effects, making the application easier to debug and maintain.

2. Pure Functions

Redux reducers are pure functions. This means the same input (state and action) will always produce the same output (new state), with no side effects. Functional programming encourages writing pure functions that avoid mutable state, making it easier to reason about code.

Example: A pure reducer in Redux might look like this:
javascript
Copy code

```javascript
function addItem(state, item) {
  return { ...state, items: [...state.items, item] };
}
```

Here, addItem is a pure function because it does not mutate the state or rely on any external variables or side effects.

3. Higher-Order Functions and Reducer Composition

Functional programming encourages the use of higher-order functions (functions that take other functions as arguments or return them). This can be particularly useful when composing multiple reducers or actions in Redux.

Example: In Redux, you can use combineReducers, which is essentially a higher-order function that takes multiple reducer functions and combines them into one reducer function.

```javascript
Copy code
import { combineReducers } from 'redux';

const rootReducer = combineReducers({
  counter: counterReducer,
```

items: itemsReducer

});

In this example, combineReducers allows you to split the application's state management into separate pieces (e.g., counter and items) while keeping the reducers modular and composable.

4. Declarative State Updates

Functional programming encourages writing declarative code, which describes what the program should do, rather than how to do it. Redux allows you to express state transitions in a declarative way, using action creators and reducer functions to describe the desired state change.

Example: A declarative action creator in Redux might look like this:

javascript
Copy code
```javascript
const increment = () => ({ type: 'INCREMENT' });
const decrement = () => ({ type: 'DECREMENT' });
```

In this case, increment and decrement describe the action in a simple, declarative way, while the reducer handles the actual state update.

5. Using Middleware for Side Effects

In functional programming, side effects (like API calls, logging, or interacting with external systems) are often managed separately from the core logic. In Redux, middleware such as redux-thunk or redux-saga allows you to handle side effects functionally, keeping your reducers pure and isolated from any asynchronous code.

Example: Using redux-thunk, you can dispatch functions that perform asynchronous actions and then dispatch other actions based on the results.

```javascript
Copy code
function fetchData() {
  return function (dispatch) {
    dispatch({ type: 'FETCH_START' });
    fetch('/api/data')
      .then(response => response.json())
```

```
        .then(data    =>    dispatch({    type:
'FETCH_SUCCESS', payload: data }))
    .catch(error => dispatch({ type: 'FETCH_ERROR',
error }));
  };
}
```

Here, the fetchData action creator is a higher-order function that dispatches actions based on asynchronous events, making it easy to separate concerns and maintain a clean, functional structure.

6. Functional Composition

Functional composition is the process of combining simple functions to create more complex functionality. In Redux, you can compose functions to build more flexible and reusable code.

Example: You can compose action creators, reducers, and middleware functions to create a modular and reusable state management structure.

javascript
Copy code

```
const logAction = (action) => {
  console.log('Dispatching action:', action);
  return action;
};

const rootReducer = combineReducers({
  counter: counterReducer,
  items: itemsReducer
});

const store = createStore(
  rootReducer,
  applyMiddleware(logAction)
);
```

In this case, logAction is a higher-order function that wraps the dispatch process with logging, demonstrating function composition in action.

7. Declarative UI with Redux and Functional Programming

When you integrate Redux with a functional-reactive programming (FRP) approach, you can declaratively manage UI state updates in your components. By mapping Redux state to props and dispatching actions based on user interactions, you maintain a clear separation between logic and UI.

Example: With React-Redux, you can use the connect function to map Redux state and dispatch to the component's props.

```javascript
Copy code
import { connect } from 'react-redux';

const Counter = ({ counter, increment, decrement }) => (
  <div>
    <p>{counter}</p>
    <button onClick={increment}>Increment</button>
                                          <button onClick={decrement}>Decrement</button>
  </div>
);

const mapStateToProps = state => ({
  counter: state.counter
});
```

```
const mapDispatchToProps = dispatch => ({
  increment: () => dispatch({ type: 'INCREMENT' }),
  decrement: () => dispatch({ type: 'DECREMENT' })
});

export default connect(mapStateToProps, mapDispatchToProps)(Counter);
```

Here, the component is purely declarative, relying on Redux for state management and using mapStateToProps and mapDispatchToProps to handle updates functionally.

Conclusion

Using Redux with functional programming patterns helps you write cleaner, more maintainable, and predictable code by adhering to principles like immutability, pure functions, and composition. By embracing higher-order functions, middleware for side effects, and declarative approaches, you can build powerful and scalable applications that are easier to manage and debug.

Chapter 15

Functional Programming in Real-world JavaScript

Functional programming (FP) has practical applications in real-world JavaScript projects, especially as modern JavaScript frameworks and libraries support and promote functional paradigms. By using FP principles—like immutability, pure functions, and function composition—developers can build maintainable, testable, and reusable code.

In real-world scenarios, functional programming is often used in managing state, handling data transformations, and processing asynchronous operations. For example, libraries like Redux use immutability and pure functions to handle complex application states predictably. Array methods such as map, filter, and reduce offer powerful data manipulation tools, while higher-order functions like compose and pipe streamline complex logic by allowing developers to create pipelines of functions.

Additionally, React encourages functional patterns by promoting stateless, reusable components, especially with hooks like useState and useEffect, which can be combined for composable, functional UI code. Asynchronous work can also be handled functionally through Promises and async/await, which make functional approaches to error handling and chaining operations straightforward.

By applying these FP practices, JavaScript applications become more resilient, scalable, and easier to understand, significantly benefiting both frontend and backend development.

Real-world Use Cases

Functional programming (FP) finds extensive applications in real-world JavaScript development. Its principles of immutability, pure functions, and declarative code structure make it particularly well-suited for various tasks. Here are some key use cases:

1. Data Transformation and Processing

FP is often used for transforming and processing data efficiently. Methods like map, filter, and reduce allow developers to handle arrays and objects in a clean, readable, and functional way. For example, transforming API response data into a usable format or filtering records based on specific criteria are common tasks.

2. State Management

State management tools like Redux leverage functional principles such as immutability and pure reducers. By managing state in a functional way, developers can ensure predictability and maintainability in applications, especially in complex, large-scale systems.

3. Asynchronous Workflows

Handling asynchronous operations with Promises and async/await allows for functional chaining and cleaner error handling. Libraries like RxJS use functional reactive programming to manage streams of data in real-time applications such as chat apps or live dashboards.

4. Reusable UI Components

In frameworks like React, FP encourages the creation of stateless functional components. These components are reusable and easier to test, contributing to modular and maintainable user interfaces.

5. Error Handling and Validation

Functional programming techniques such as Either, Maybe, or Option types help manage errors and handle edge cases gracefully, minimizing runtime errors and improving code robustness.

6. Functional Utilities in Libraries

Libraries like Lodash and Ramda provide FP utilities that simplify tasks like function composition, currying, and working with collections. These tools are invaluable in real-world applications where code needs to be reusable and concise.

7. Domain-Specific Logic

FP is often applied in areas like financial calculations, data analytics, and scientific computations, where pure functions ensure accurate, predictable outcomes, and immutability avoids unintended side effects.

Functional programming in JavaScript is not just a theoretical concept but a practical approach that enhances reliability, scalability, and developer productivity in real-world applications.

Performance Considerations

While functional programming (FP) promotes cleaner and more maintainable code, it can introduce performance trade-offs if not implemented thoughtfully. Understanding these considerations is key to balancing functional principles with efficiency.

1. Immutability Overhead

Immutability requires creating new data structures instead of modifying existing ones. This can lead to increased memory usage and garbage collection pressure, particularly in applications that frequently manipulate large datasets. Persistent data structures and libraries like Immutable.js can mitigate these issues.

2. Recursive Function Calls

Recursion, a common pattern in FP, may result in stack overflow errors or inefficient execution compared to iterative loops. Tail call optimization (TCO), supported in some JavaScript engines, can help reduce the performance overhead of recursion by reusing stack frames for recursive calls.

3. Higher-order Function Costs

Higher-order functions like map, filter, and reduce abstract control flow but may have performance overhead compared to manual loops, especially in performance-critical code. Optimizing these functions with careful chaining or using transducers can improve efficiency.

4. Garbage Collection

Functional patterns that rely heavily on temporary objects (e.g., chaining array operations) may increase garbage collection frequency, which could impact performance in memory-intensive applications.

5. Lazy Evaluation

Lazy evaluation, a feature in some functional programming libraries, defers computation until necessary. While this can improve performance in certain cases, excessive reliance on laziness might complicate debugging and memory management. Libraries like Lodash with lazy functions can help balance performance.

6. Parallelism and Asynchronous Processing

FP's declarative nature can align well with parallel and asynchronous processing, such as with Promises, async/await, or libraries like RxJS. By structuring code functionally, workloads can be distributed more effectively across threads or asynchronous tasks.

7. Benchmarking and Profiling

To ensure performance remains acceptable, developers should regularly benchmark and profile their functional code. Tools like Chrome DevTools and libraries like Benchmark.js can identify bottlenecks introduced by functional abstractions.

8. Choosing the Right Approach

For performance-critical sections, blending functional and imperative paradigms may be necessary. For example, using a manual loop instead of reduce might yield significant spccdups without sacrificing maintainability elsewhere in the code.

By recognizing these considerations and leveraging JavaScript's flexibility as a multi-paradigm language, developers can write functional code that balances performance and clarity effectively.

Best Practices for Large-scale Functional JavaScript

Functional programming (FP) can bring structure, reusability, and maintainability to large JavaScript applications. Adopting certain best practices ensures that functional principles work effectively at scale. Here are key best practices to follow:

1. Embrace Immutability

Immutability helps prevent side effects, making code easier to reason about and debug. Use libraries like Immutable.js or native Object.freeze for complex data structures. Embracing immutability in state management, particularly in applications like Redux, ensures that changes are predictable and traceable.

2. Use Pure Functions for Consistency

Pure functions, which depend only on inputs and produce no side effects, make applications easier to test, reuse, and scale. Breaking down code into small, focused pure functions enables reliable composition and reduces coupling, allowing changes in one part of the code without impacting others.

3. Leverage Higher-order Functions

Higher-order functions (like map, filter, and reduce) and custom higher-order functions can abstract common logic patterns. These functions encourage reusability by allowing developers to write generalized solutions applicable to various situations without duplicating code.

4. Adopt Function Composition

Function composition combines simple functions into more complex ones, enabling clean, declarative code. Libraries like Ramda provide utilities for composing functions (e.g., compose, pipe), which simplify the chaining of transformations, especially in data pipelines.

5. Use Currying and Partial Application

Currying and partial application allow for more flexible and reusable functions by breaking them down into smaller, parameterized functions. Currying enables function reuse by allowing you to pass in only some arguments and get a new function that waits for the remaining arguments.

6. Organize Code into Modules

Modularize code into well-defined units that align with the application's domain logic. Each module should contain related functions, utilities, or components. Using named exports, instead of default ones, improves clarity when importing and makes it easier to manage dependencies.

7. Manage State Functionally

State management is critical in large applications, and managing it functionally helps prevent unpredictable behaviors. Libraries like Redux and RxJS support functional state management with predictable flows and pure reducers, helping applications remain scalable and maintainable over time.

8. Minimize Side Effects and Use Controlled Side Effects

FP emphasizes reducing side effects, but in large applications, they're sometimes unavoidable (e.g., API calls, DOM updates). Use controlled side effects by isolating them in specific functions (e.g., in async functions or Redux middleware). Keep side effects outside of core logic to avoid coupling, allowing easier testing and debugging.

9. Utilize Lazy Evaluation for Efficiency

Lazy evaluation, available in libraries like Lodash, helps avoid unnecessary computations by deferring execution until needed. It's especially beneficial when working with large data structures where processing only required elements can significantly improve performance.

10. Prioritize Readability and Maintainability

Functional code should remain readable and maintainable. Avoid overusing chaining or complex compositions that might obscure intent. Name intermediate steps in a chain and use helper functions if it aids in clarity. Document functions to clarify their behavior, especially if they involve advanced functional concepts.

11. Embrace Testing and Debugging Practices

Large functional applications are easier to test due to the predictability of pure functions and immutability. Ensure comprehensive testing for each function, particularly with edge cases, and use tools like Jest or Mocha. Debugging tools like Chrome DevTools and performance profiling can help identify bottlenecks and ensure the functional code runs efficiently.

12. Adopt Functional Patterns for Async Operations

Asynchronous operations can be handled functionally with Promises, async/await, and libraries like RxJS for reactive programming. Functional patterns make asynchronous workflows predictable and easier to reason about, especially in large-scale applications with complex data flows.

By following these practices, developers can harness the benefits of functional programming in large JavaScript applications while maintaining performance, readability, and scalability

www.ingramcontent.com/pod-product-compliance
Lightning Source LLC
LaVergne TN
LVHW051429050326
832903LV00030BD/2993